# Cambridge Elements ≡

Elements in Psychology and Culture
edited by
Kenneth D. Keith
*University of San Diego*

# WOMEN ACROSS CULTURES

## *Common Issues, Varied Experiences*

Hilary M. Lips
*Radford University*

CAMBRIDGE
UNIVERSITY PRESS

# CAMBRIDGE
## UNIVERSITY PRESS

University Printing House, Cambridge CB2 8BS, United Kingdom

One Liberty Plaza, 20th Floor, New York, NY 10006, USA

477 Williamstown Road, Port Melbourne, VIC 3207, Australia

314–321, 3rd Floor, Plot 3, Splendor Forum, Jasola District Centre,
New Delhi – 110025, India

79 Anson Road, #06–04/06, Singapore 079906

Cambridge University Press is part of the University of Cambridge.

It furthers the University's mission by disseminating knowledge in the pursuit of
education, learning, and research at the highest international levels of excellence.

www.cambridge.org
Information on this title: www.cambridge.org/9781108812788
DOI: 10.1017/9781108874366

© Hilary M. Lips 2021

First published 2021

*A catalogue record for this publication is available from the British Library.*

ISBN 978-1-108-81278-8 Paperback
ISSN 2515-3986 (online)
ISSN 2515-3943 (print)

# Women across Cultures

## Common Issues, Varied Experiences

Elements in Psychology and Culture

DOI: 10.1017/9781108874366
First published online: February 2021

Hilary M. Lips
*Radford University*
Author for correspondence: Hilary M. Lips, hlips@radford.edu

**Abstract:** Psychology's study of women has revealed some themes that span cultures and countries, yet women's lived experiences in different cultures can be dramatically different. This Element explores, from a psychological perspective, women's issues in cultural contexts. Beginning with the question of public and private identity (i.e., who "counts" as a woman), it goes on to examine embodiment, sexuality, reproduction, family roles, economic participation and power, violence, leadership, and feminist activism. It concludes with a brief discussion of women's complicated relationship to culture: as both keepers and sometimes prisoners of cultural traditions – particularly in the context of migration to different cultures. Running through the Element are two general themes: the pervasiveness of a gender hierarchy that often privileges men over women, and the ways in which women's lived experience varies within cultures according to the intersection of gender with other categories that affect expectations, norms, power, and privilege.

**Keywords:** women, gender, sexuality, motherhood, leadership, discrimination

ISBNs: 9781108812788 (PB), 9781108874366 (OC)
ISSNs: 2515-3986 (online), 2515-3943 (print)

# Contents

# 1 Introduction

The first part of the twenty-first century has been, in many ways, a watershed period for women. In many parts of the world, women have signaled collectively that they will resist and challenge long-standing traditions that have often kept them politically, socially, and economically marginalized. The vocal and global #MeToo movement has brought scrutiny and punishment to the actions of powerful men who heretofore often harassed and bullied female colleagues with impunity. A young woman, Greta Thunberg, is the international face of environmental activism. In India, five million women formed a 385-mile human wall of protest to support gender equality (Poonam, 2019). Women's percentage of seats in national legislative bodies rose from 18 percent in 2008 to 25 percent in 2020 (Atske, Geiger, & Scheller, 2019; World Economic Forum, 2019). Worldwide, the gaps between women and men in educational attainment and in health and survival have narrowed significantly, although gaps in political empowerment and economic participation are still considerable (World Economic Forum, 2019).

The year 2020 marks the twenty-fifth anniversary of the historic Beijing *Fourth World Conference on Women*, which set out a platform for international action based on a vision of gender equality. In the United States, where 2020 marks the hundredth anniversary of women's suffrage, women's representation in legislative bodies is at an all-time high, and several women have made credible runs for the presidency. In Europe, high-profile female leaders hold important economic posts: Ursula von der Lyen presides over the European Commission, Christine Lagarde leads the European Central Bank, and Kristalina Georgieva serves as Managing Director of the International Monetary Fund. Women hold the office of Prime Minister in four of the five Nordic countries. The African Women Leaders Network, which works to advance female leaders and to develop policies that empower women across the continent, was launched to much fanfare in 2017. In Kenya, Sophia Abdi Noor, the first female member of Parliament elected from Northeastern Kenya, has emphatically devoted her political career to advocating for the rights of marginalized women. At this writing, women hold international posts as the United Nations High Commissioner for Human Rights (Michele Bachelet), Director-General of UNESCO (Audrey Azoulay), Executive Director of UNICEF (Henrietta Fore), Executive Director of the United Nations Population Fund (Natalia Kanem), Executive Director of UNAIDS (Winnie Byanyima), President and CEO of Save the Children (Janti Soeripto), and NATO Secretary-General's Special Representative for Women, Peace, and Security (Claire Hutchinson).

Yet, even as some clarity seems to be emerging about women and their place in societies – when antiquated stereotypes are starting to evaporate and brittle justifications for women's second-class status are crumbling – it appears that "change has been agonizingly slow for the majority of women and girls in the world ... [and] ... not a single country can claim to have achieved gender equality" (UN Women, 2019). Furthermore, a new question has emerged to muddy that clarity: Who counts as a woman?

## 2 Who Counts as a Woman?: Public and Private Identity

Suffragist Susan B. Anthony certainly thought of herself as a woman. Indeed, she devoted her adult life laser-focused on the struggle to secure rights for women. Yet, one of the many insults thrown at her by her adversaries in that struggle was that she was not a real woman. One detractor called her "an ungainly hermaphrodite, part male, part female, with an ugly face and shrill voice" (quoted in Baker, 2005, p. 63). Women in leadership positions frequently face labels and stereotypes that impugn their femininity (e.g., Hall & Donaghue, 2013; Lips, 2000) and they elicit feelings of masculinity threat in men (Netchaeva, Kouchaki, & Sheppard, 2015).

Gender-based insults are widely used and have been shown to sting (e.g., Rowe, 2014). Threats to femininity or masculinity can generate behavior designed to compensate and to shore up gender identity among people who identify as women or men (Gordon & Glass, 1970; Sinclair, Carlsson, & Björklund, 2016; van Veelen, Derks, & Endedijk, 2019; Willer et al., 2013). Such threats challenge an individual's legitimacy as a member of a binary category that has traditionally been assigned huge significance. However, a small but insistent number of people refuse to accept the importance of such categories or to claim membership in one of these binary categories as key to their identity. In a large Australian study, 7.75 percent of respondents selected a nonbinary option (rather than woman or man) when asked to indicate their gender (Whyte, Brooks, & Torgler, 2018). One group of researchers who explored gender identity in a large sample of adults in Israel found that fully 35 percent of respondents felt to some extent as both genders or neither, and concluded that "the current view of gender identity as binary and unitary does not reflect the experience of many individuals" (Joel et al., 2014, p. 291). Individuals' refusal to accept a binary, nonoverlapping view of gender/sex in terms of identity and behavior is not unreasonable. Years of psychological research has failed to support the hypothesis of a clear sexual dimorphism of the human brain and hormonal systems, the inevitable alignment of gender identity with anatomy, and large nonoverlapping sex/gender differences in most behaviors. Research has also shown that the tendency to accept gender/sex as an important binary category is "culturally determined and malleable" (Hyde et al., 2019, p. 171).

Yet, even as people resist binary categories, these categories are consequential. Being labeled female or male affects the way an individual's behavior is evaluated, the expectations others hold for that person, and the cultural rewards and restrictions they are likely to encounter. Thus, it is not surprising that many people care, often deeply, about being "correctly" labeled or about their perceived "fit" into gender categories.

For women, in particular, the question of public gender identity and its implications may be nuanced and fluid, and associated with age. For certain purposes, women's public status as female may be limited to their reproductive years. For instance, the Hindu temple of Sabarimala in Kerala, India has traditionally been closed to all women of menstruating age because menstruation was thought to render them impure. In 2018, crowds of protestors attacked women who tried to enter. India's Supreme Court had earlier ruled that women had the right to enter the temple – but the angry mob outside made it impossible for even a single female devotee to enter (Clayton, 2018).

Young girls and old women are not necessarily counted as women and sometimes face fewer restrictions associated with femininity. In many cultures, girls are allowed to "run wild" until they approach puberty – when they are pressured to begin dressing and acting in conventional feminine ways (Carr, 2007; Currie, 1997; Hyde & Jaffee, 2000; Shakib, 2003). In some Muslim societies, although there is wide variation, girls do not begin wearing a veil until puberty; in others, some women stop veiling after menopause (Huda, 2019). In North America, movements (e.g., the Red Hat Society) are afoot among some older women to break free of the necessity to conform to the more demure expectations associated with femininity.

Some North American psychological research suggests that the impact of the transition to puberty on young women's self-concept is experienced as restrictive and diminishing (Brown & Gilligan, 1992; Pipher, 1994; Piran, 2016; 2017). If so, girls' construction of a private and public identity as a woman may be fraught with disadvantages. Yet, having made that transition, they clearly "count" as women.

Older women, perhaps because they are viewed as asexual, often feel invisible and uncounted as women (Altschuler, 2017; Lemish & Muhlbauer, 2012). Events organized for women often focus on those younger than sixty-five; even statistics on women often omit consideration of older women.

Competitive sport is one arena that shows the clear failure of a simple dichotomous system for categorizing people as female or male. Even after years of controversy and research, there is no satisfactory answer to the question, "what makes a person female or male for purposes of athletic competition?" Athletes who identify as women have sometimes faced barriers to being counted as women if their physiques do not seem to fall within the range of the prototypical female body or if their performance is unusually impressive. In 2018, the IOC and IAAF instituted rules that bar women with high testosterone levels from competing as women in races of 400 meters to one mile. If a woman's testosterone level is within the male range, she is barred from competing as a woman. The only allowable exceptions are for women whose bodies are insensitive to testosterone or for those who agree to reduce their testosterone through medical means. This rule impacts, among others, Castor Semenya, the South African champion in the women's 800 meters.

Finally, discussions about the gender binary have sometimes been complicated by the urgent voices of individuals who, although labeled as female or male at birth, feel strongly that they more properly belong to the other category – and want to be counted as such. The argument here is not so much that gender should not be a rigid binary but that it *is* a binary – and individuals care deeply about the category into which they fit. Arguments around this issue have been contentious and painful. When Caitlyn Jenner, a transgender woman who presented an extremely glamorous and ultra-feminine public image, was named 2015 "Woman of the Year" by *Glamour Magazine*, some commentators protested that she was not a "real" woman. Transgender students in schools may face restrictions on their use of sex-segregated bathrooms and locker rooms that correspond to their gender identity (Kralik, 2016). Women's colleges have struggled to develop policies on whether to admit transgender students (North, 2017). Even some feminist groups, whose overarching aim is often to diminish sex/gender as a limiting category, have had uncomfortable debates about whether transwomen should be included as women (Lee, 2010). These debates underline the complexities in defining the category "woman" – and perhaps it is not possible to agree completely on what qualities are necessary and sufficient to define this category.

One key aspect of the experience of being female is the label itself. As decades of psychological research have shown, a person labeled as female evokes certain assumptions, reactions, and expectations. These differ across cultures but there is no culture where the label is inconsequential, where persons categorized as women and men are treated in exactly the same ways. Women's life experience and sense of self is shaped by the cultural expectations that attend their categorization as women. Another important aspect of femaleness is the private experience of the body, such as awareness of the possibility of pregnancy, anxiety over infertility, monthly concerns and practices around menstruation, disquiet over the risk of breast cancer, and worry over projecting an acceptable physical appearance of femininity. Not every woman shares all these experiences and they can mean different things in different cultural contexts. Yet, the idea that womanhood is at least partly defined by the female body is underlined by the lengths to which individuals go to fit their bodies to a female ideal and by the extraordinary efforts made by many transgender persons to achieve a body that matches their identity.

Consideration of the differences among women in terms of their experiences of societal expectations and of their bodies leads inevitably to the acknowledgment of intersectionality (Crenshaw, 1991). There is no such thing as a "pure" experience of womanhood, where being categorized as and identifying as female is the only relevant factor in determining an individual's social identity and experience. Factors such as race, ethnicity, class, culture, nationality, age, sexual orientation, gender identity, and ability intertwine with gender, such that what it means and how it feels to be a woman is different in various combinations of these dimensions. (And, conversely, what it means to be Black or poor or old or to have a disability is different, depending on one's gender category.)

Given these complications, how are we to decide who "counts" as a woman? A purely biological definition of womanhood (chromosomes) would omit androgen-insensitive individuals. A definition based on the capacity for childbearing would leave out women who cannot become pregnant. A definition based purely on identity includes people who may not share either the body or the bulk of experiences that many women claim as uniquely feminine. For the purpose of this Element, the category "woman" includes all who identify as and try to live as women. However, I make this decision with the understanding that gender categories are fuzzy and fluid at best, that not everyone reaches their gender identity via the same route, and that there are deep disagreements about inclusion in the category "woman" (e.g., Burkett, 2015). In this Element, I attempt not only to show the common threads in diverse women's experiences but also the differences among women.

## 3 Embodying Femininity: Issues of Beauty, Strength, Youth

One aspect of normative femininity that prevails across cultures is the pressure to be attractive (e.g., Beale, Malson, & Tischner, 2016; Fiaveh et al., 2015). Indeed, some have suggested that "femininity is … constructed as a bodily practice" (Riley & Scharff, 2013, p. 207), and sexist insults directed at women are highly likely to demean their appearance (e.g., Felmlee, Inara Rodis, & Zhang, 2019). Whereas cultures differ in what particular qualities they deem attractive for women (e.g., Docan-Morgan, 2016; Kleisner et al., 2017), the enforcement of beauty norms is a common thread.

Women in Western, developed cultures are exhorted to strive for thinness (which is associated with control, wealth, and happiness), while individuals in non-Western, poorer cultures may link thinness with poverty, disease, and malnutrition, and thus admire larger women. In this respect, the desirability of different images may also be racially charged within cultures. For example, in one study, Black Canadian adolescents noted that they were sometimes criticized both within and outside their communities for being skinny "like . . . those starving children with the big stomachs in the World Vision commercial" (Rice, 2014, p. 247) – a criticism that would not be made of a similarly thin young White woman. There are also indications that larger body size is more acceptable and less stigmatized in Black American communities (Hicken et al., 2013).

The increasing "westernization" of many cultures may have shrunk the gap between cultural preferences with respect to weight (Anderson-Fye, 2004; Grogan, 2008; Swami, 2015). One large cross-national study (Swami et al., 2010) revealed only minor differences in ideals for the female figure and in female body dissatisfaction among high-socioeconomic (SES) sites. By comparison, heavier bodies were preferred in some low-SES sites. Women's body dissatisfaction was associated with their exposure to Western media – a finding congruent with other cross-cultural studies (e.g., Becker et al., 2002; Swami et al., 2014; Ting & Hwang, 2007). Similarly, female immigrants to Western cultures who acculturate and internalize those beauty standards are likely to experience body dissatisfaction (Poloskov & Tracey, 2013). Social media use is also implicated in body dissatisfaction. In Korea and the United States, women's use of social media for information about body image is negatively related to body satisfaction (Lee et al., 2014); among young Chinese women, posting selfies on a social networking site is linked to restrained eating (Niu et al., 2020).

In contexts where women do not internalize Western media representations of beauty, or where women wear clothing specifically designed to conceal their bodies, they may express less body dissatisfaction (Dunkel, Davidson, & Qurashi, 2009). For example, one study of Muslim women in France revealed that those who wore the hijab reported less body dissatisfaction and drive for thinness (but more discrimination) than did their non-hijab-wearing counterparts (Kertechian & Swami, 2016). However, even in countries such as Iran, which enforce concealment-oriented dress for women, women fret about their size and weight (Alqout & Reynolds, 2014; Nikniaz et al., 2016). One study found that about one-third of Iranian adolescent girls sampled had attempted to lose weight (Garousi et al., 2016).

Body dissatisfaction can arise from sources other than body weight, and cultures differ in the priorities placed on different dimensions of female beauty. A study of Thai women found that facial appearance (bright skin, big eyes, high nose bridge), was more salient to body satisfaction than body weight and shape (Rongmuang et al., 2011). Similarly, while body size and shape are viewed as important, dissatisfaction with the face was also significantly correlated with overall body dissatisfaction among female adolescents in Australia, China, and Malaysia (Mellor et al., 2013),

Feminist theories predict that women within cultures where there is rapidly increasing equality in gender roles will experience greater body dissatisfaction – because backlash against women's advances may include more pressure to conform to beauty ideals. Support for this prediction is mixed. Consistent with feminist theory, Korean women (living in a culture changing rapidly toward increasingly equal gender roles) reported more body dissatisfaction than did women in the United States and China (Jung & Forbes, 2007; Jung, Forbes, & Lee, 2009). However, women in Brazil and Argentina, where social change has also been rapid and unsettling, did not show higher levels of body dissatisfaction than US women did (Forbes et al., 2012).

It has been argued that the beauty practices that stem from enforcement of appearance ideals helps to maintain the subordination of women – that the enactment of femininity implied in the molding of one's appearance to fit these cultural standards is an enactment of female subordination (Jeffreys, 2005). Objectification theory posits that body standards are tools for oppressing women – by making women feel unacceptable and inadequate as they are, by pushing them to spend their time, attention, energy, and money on attempts to meet these body standards, and by manipulating them to engage in such beauty practices in order to please the dominant group: men (Fredrickson & Roberts, 1997). On the other hand, some analysts have suggested that women's beauty practices often express agency and strategy: taking control of their appearance in the interests of self-expression or exerting influence (e.g., Bae, 2011; Scott, 2005). As Felski (2006) has noted, both approaches probably capture aspects of women's beauty practices. Rice (2014), reporting on an interview study of diverse women aged twenty to forty-five, has argued for a nuanced approach, noting that her respondents indicated awareness both of the cultural pressures related to appearance and of the pleasure and other advantages linked to shaping their appearance in particular ways.

Body dissatisfaction that stems from the cultural enforcement of beauty ideals for women has been implicated in eating disorders and distressing body management practices (Blood, 2005; Malson, 1998). Pressure to conform to beauty ideals often comes from public or social media. One often-cited study involves the impact on young women in Fiji of the introduction of Western television (Becker et al., 2002). Indicators of disordered eating, such as dieting and vomiting to lose weight, increased after the girls' exposure to television. Studies in many countries have shown a link between women's body dissatisfaction, disordered eating, and exposure to mass media portrayals of physical attractiveness. Body dissatisfaction and disordered eating have been linked to perceived appearance pressure from mass media in Australia (Hargreaves & Tiggemann, 2004), North America (Rogers Wood, Nikel, & Petrie, 2010; Shroff & Thompson, 2006), Europe (Girard, Rodgers, & Chabrol, 2018; Knauss, Paxton, & Alsaker, 2008), Brazil (Amaral & Ferreira, 2017), and China (Jackson, Jiang, & Chen, 2016). For women, the association between media appearance pressure and body dissatisfaction appears to be mediated in part by making upward appearance-related social comparisons (Luo et al., 2020). In cultures where women are constantly exposed to images of very thin women, women make numerous upward social comparisons daily, thus increasing body dissatisfaction (Leahey, Crowther, & Mickelson, 2007).

In constructions of femininity, beauty is often entangled with constraint, weakness, and fragility. For instance, the emphasis on high heels in some cultural contexts helps to maintain an image of women as tiny, unstable, and restricted in their movements (Burcar, 2018). This harkens back to the traditional Chinese practice of binding women's feet, rendering them all but crippled in the service of beauty standards that included tiny "lotus feet" (Malchik, 2020). Indeed, feminine fragility has been used in various cultural contexts to "protect" women from participating in dangerous or labor-intensive jobs and as an excuse to restrict their movements (e.g., Bhalerao, 2019). However, the high media visibility and popularity of demonstrably strong female athletes such as Serena Williams and Megan Rapinoe may have helped somewhat to modify the link between femininity and weakness. Female athletes are aware that their athleticism is viewed as a deviation from femininity and that they are seen as different from "normal" women. On the other hand, they also express pride in their strong bodies and a sense of empowerment that extends beyond the context of their sports (Krane et al., 2004).

Social scientists have noted that women's self-worth is likely more "embodied" than men's – that by the time women reach old age they have absorbed decades of judgment about their bodies that affects their self-esteem (Holstein, 2015). Aging is a normal aspect of life, and women do adjust their expectations and their comparison groups to account for physical aging (Carter, 2016; Tiggemann, 2004). Furthermore, older women may embrace a heightened salience and appreciation of body functionality and health over appearance (Tiggemann, 2015). However, the loss of youthful forms of beauty and of some easy functionality of youth can be distressing for older women in Westernized cultures. Western media promote negative attitudes about the aging female body; for example, women in the United States indicate more anxiety about aging and more concern about physical appearance changes than do women in Korea (Yun & Lachman, 2006). Negative attitudes can be found in many developed cultures.

For instance, women view other women as "old" at earlier ages than they do men in Qatar (Musaiger, D'Souza, & Al-Roomi, 2013) and old women are more negatively stereotyped than old men in Sweden (Oberg & Tornstam, 2003).

Across cultures, then, women experience pressure to fit their bodies to often-unattainable standards of attractiveness. The particularities of such standards vary across cultural contexts but the importance of bodily appearance to constructions of femininity is pervasive.

## 4 Sexuality and Reproduction

The cultural focus on women's bodies and physical appearance is grounded in the power that is linked to sexuality and reproduction – and cultural attempts to control that power by controlling women. The biological processes of reproduction – menstruation, pregnancy, childbirth, lactation – are obvious in women and thus provide both motivation and opportunity for control of women. Historically, many cultures have surrounded women's reproductive processes with myths, rituals, and taboos. For example, some Native American cultures regarded menstruating women as so powerful that they must stay away from men preparing for battle, lest their power interfere with the warriors' power (Allen, 1986). In Nepal, a few young women still die every year because, considered impure, they have been compelled to seclude themselves in isolated huts away from their communities during their menstrual period (Gettelman, 2018). The onset of menstruation, with its implication that pregnancy is now a possibility, triggers new parental concerns and behavioral restrictions on young women in many cultures – from emphasis on modest dress and on distancing from males to increased parental control and admonitions about sexual vulnerability (e.g., Golchin et al., 2012; Grant, 2012; Herbert et al., 2017).

One way in which women's sexuality is controlled is via a double standard for appropriate heterosexual behavior – an ideology that excuses or even commends men but condemns women for high sexual activity or promiscuity (e.g., Marks, Young, & Zaikman, 2019; Tolman & Chmielewski, 2019). Whereas this ideology exists in many cultures, it is not universal. Respondents in countries with greater gender equality endorse the double standard less strongly (Endendijk, van Baar, & Deković, 2020). Furthermore, it does not appear to be an important factor all cultures. For example, the following comments by Nisa, the !Kung woman interviewed at length by anthropologist Marjorie Shostak (1981), revealed no hint of disapproval for women's indulgence of their sexual desires:

> [W]hen you are a woman, you don't just sit still and do nothing – you have lovers. You don't just sit with the man of your hut, with just one man. One

man can give you very little. ... All women know sexual pleasure. Some women, those who really like sex, if they haven't finished and the man has, will wait until the man has rested, then get up and make love to him. Because she wants to finish too. She'll have sex with the man until she is also satisfied. Otherwise she could get sick. (pp. 271, 287)

In many cultures, however, young women struggle to balance sexual agency and empowerment with negative appraisals that paint sexually active women as damaged and/or immoral. In Western cultures, celebrities and social media influencers sometimes promote sexual agency for women. A well-known example is top-ranked entertainer Beyoncé, who is intentionally and aggressively sexual in her performances and who argues strongly that women should claim their sexuality. She asserts that a woman can "be a businesswoman, a mother, an artist, and a feminist – and still be a sexual being. It's not mutually exclusive" (quoted in Hicklin, 2014). From this perspective, young women may be encouraged to feel that they should acknowledge their own sexual needs and not let traditional social norms inhibit them from engaging in sexual relationships if they desire them. Indeed, research among college students in the United States suggests that most women say they are motivated to participate in casual sexual encounters because of sexual desire or physical gratification (Fielder & Carey, 2010). However, cultural norms restricting women's sexuality still have an impact: women in this group are more likely than are young men to regret casual sexual encounters. This regret is linked to the perception of a loss of respect from their partner, loss of self-respect, the feeling that they were pressured or forced, and a low level of sexual enjoyment (Uecker & Martinez, 2017). Even though they feel more empowered to be sexually active than in the past, young women in the United States are more likely than are young men to feel negatively judged for participating in casual sex (Kettrey, 2016). The level of regulation and potential disapproval that surrounds sexuality, particularly women's sexuality, mark the United States as a sex-negative country (Interligi & McHugh, 2018). Within such a cultural context, young women may find sexual empowerment to be a double-edged sword (Lamb & Peterson, 2012).

In many cultural contexts, however, the notion of sexual agency for women is not acceptable or even debatable. Women may be disowned or severely sanctioned by their families and communities for behavior that is perceived as too sexual – even if such behavior does not involve any sexual activity at all, but simply spending time with men, dressing immodestly in public spaces, or going unchaperoned into certain situations. Such behavior violates societal (and sometimes religious) norms that dictate that women should be pure and that may link a family's honor to a daughter's behavior. Even in very restrictive cultures, however, some women find covert ways to exert agency by engaging in deliberately transgressive practices. Young Saudi Arabian women may routinely and intentionally violate the rules of modest dress (Le Renard, 2013), take the initiative in flirting with men they do not know by sending Bluetooth signals from their smartphones (Marketplace.org, 2008), or pursue romance via social media outlets such as Snapchat and Facebook (Naylor, 2016). Women may push back even further against restrictions. For example, in Iran, premarital sex among young women has increased over the past two decades and young women have sometimes been viewed as leading a sexual revolution in that country (Mahdavi, 2009). However, these young women, though defiant in certain ways, are reportedly more fearful of the social risks of sexual activity, such as being caught by the Islamic morality police or by their families, than of health risks such as contracting sexually transmitted infections. Thus, although sexually active, they may be afraid to access information, contraception, resources for testing, and treatment for such infections. In such a case, sexual agency can be a mixed blessing.

The impact of the sexual double standard is revealed in extreme form in cultural settings where female rape survivors are blamed rather than believed by their communities (e.g., Munala et al., 2018) and even rejected by their families. However, it is evident, though more subtle, in the patterns of victim blaming that vary according to culture but persist across many. For example, when presented with a case of marital rape, respondents from Turkey, a culture that emphasizes male honor, blamed the victim and exonerated the perpetrator more than did respondents from Germany or Britain. However, in all three cultures, respondents were more likely to blame the victim and exonerate the perpetrator when the violence was in response to a threat to the husband's reputation (Gul & Schuster, 2020).

When women violate societal norms with respect to either heterosexuality or binary gender identity, social sanctions are also severe. For example, in the United States, the most common reason for homelessness among lesbian, gay, bisexual, and transgender youth is rejection by their families (Keuroghlian, Shtasel, & Bassuk, 2014). Across the globe, researchers have found negative attitudes toward both lesbian women and gay men, although gay men tend to be rated more negatively in most countries (Bettinsoli, Suppes, & Napier, 2019). Globally, transgender persons are targets of disproportionate levels of stigma, discrimination, and violence (Reisner et al., 2016). These negative reactions are linked to the perception that gay, lesbian, and transgender individuals are violating or blurring traditional gender norms with respect to heterosexuality and/or binary gender identity. Furthermore, structural stigma (discriminatory laws and policies and community attitudes) appear to explain about 60 percent of variation among countries in the life satisfaction of sexual minority individuals (Pachankis & Bränström, 2018).

Traditionally, controlling women's sexuality has been linked to controlling their reproduction. In anthropological and evolutionary accounts, a man ensures his paternity of any offspring by ensuring that his female partner is sexually monogamous with him. For example, researchers in West African countries have shown that female genital cutting is linked to the desire to reduce paternity uncertainty (e.g., Howard & Gibson, 2019). Thus, restricting women's sexuality serves the very direct purpose of controlling their reproduction, and therefore protecting a man from unknowingly devoting resources to rearing a child that was not biologically his.

However, the converse is also true: controlling women's reproduction controls their sexuality and impacts their sexual health. Women who have restricted access to contraception are more likely to seek abortions if they become pregnant (e.g., Guo et al., 2019; Obiyan & Agunbiade, 2014). According to some estimates, some 27 percent of the world's women of reproductive age live in countries where abortion is prohibited or is allowed only to save a mother's life (Center for Reproductive Rights, 2020). If a woman has no control over whether or not she becomes pregnant and/or carries a pregnancy to term, it clearly impacts her actual and experienced choices and her attitudes with respect to sexuality. For example, in one study, women's attitudes toward sexual matters became more positive after a first-trimester abortion (Bradshaw & Slade, 2007). The availability of safe, effective morning-after pills, which women can obtain and use in private, is linked with feelings of relief, satisfaction, and empowerment for both individual women and communities of women, even though such availability may take place in contexts where abortion is illegal or stigmatized (Sheldon, 2018).

As for potential mothers' attitudes toward abortion, contraception, and reproductive choice, research suggests such attitudes are nuanced and are shaped in large part by culture and context. One study of women in five European countries revealed that, although 79 percent of respondents thought that emergency contraception was a responsible choice to prevent pregnancy, almost a third of those who used it felt uncomfortable or judged when obtaining it (Nappi et al., 2013). Women who have had abortions often experience fear of social judgment, self-judgment, and a need for secrecy (Hanschmidt et al., 2016). In the United States, for example, although approximately one in four women will have an abortion, abortion is highly stigmatized, often resulting in shame or guilt. However, women who have more power and control within their intimate relationships experience less stigma after abortion (Mehta et al., 2019). Among US women who carried an unplanned pregnancy to term and then placed infants for adoption, many supported abortion as a reproductive choice – one they simply did not choose for themselves (Sisson, 2015). Young, unmarried women in Ethiopia tend to seek out illegal, clandestine abortion services in large part because of concerns over social safety – worry over the stigma of abortion and the consequences that might accrue to them from such disapproval. In choosing how to access abortion, these young women often prioritized social safety over medical safety – even though unsafe abortions are among the top five causes of maternal mortality and result in a high number of serious complications (Kebede, Middelthon, & Hilden, 2018). As one young respondent said, "Exposure of my pregnancy will cost me not only my name but also my life. If my dad finds out he will kill me" (Kebede, Middelthon, & Hilden, 2018, p. 18). Among Latina teens dealing with unintended pregnancies in California, the majority viewed neither abortion nor adoption as a possible resolution for them (even though both options were theoretically available), and reported receiving strong direction from family members and male partners about how to handle their pregnancies (Mann, Cardona, & Gómez, 2015). Among HIV positive women in Northern Vietnam, decisions about whether to continue or terminate a pregnancy were shaped through discussions with husbands, parents, siblings, and in-laws (Chi et al., 2011). Among Palestinian women, whose access to safe, legal abortion is very limited, religion and community norms were found to be central factors in affecting choices and opinions about abortion (Shahawy & Diamond, 2018).

Across cultures, then, concerns about sexuality and reproduction are key aspects of the pressures and expectations that are placed on women. Limits on reproductive choice do not appear to reduce women's sexual activity, but such limits do affect their concerns about such activity. Although pregnant women often make choices based on practical matters such as health status and economic necessity, it appears that, across cultures, social pressures such as family, community, and even political sanctions restrict such choices, often drastically, even when legal and medical restrictions are few.

## 5 Motherhood and Family Roles

Motherhood is biological in that it involves a biological link between mother and child, but motherhood is a profoundly cultural role and process. Even the physical process of labor and delivery reflects cultural attitudes and norms For example, fewer women in the United States and Canada than in other countries report walking during labor. In North America and the United Kingdom, it is standard practice for a woman's partner to be present during labor; that is not the case in Lithuania, Azerbaijan, Moldova, or St. Petersburg, Russia (Chalmers, 2012). A common scenario for childbirth in the West has the woman lying on her back with her legs spread apart, whereas the tradition in parts of Africa and elsewhere is for the woman to give birth from a kneeling position (Sudarkasa,

2004). Not surprisingly, then, women who immigrate to new cultures often encounter unfamiliar and anxiety-provoking norms and practices surrounding childbirth in their new homes (Clark, Glavin et al., 2018).

There is a pervasive idea that motherhood, and the domestic responsibilities that go with it, is a primary role for women – and that women are naturally better suited than men are to do such work. All over the world, women devote more of their time then men do to caring for children. One overview of time-use studies carried out in twenty countries between 1965 and 2003 showed that men spent an average of only fourteen minutes per day on childcare, thus leaving most of that work to women (Hook, 2006). That disparity shows some signs of shrinking. Canadian researchers have found that the percentage of total housework time contributed by men increased from 29.26% in 1986 to 41.21% in 2015, and that men's share of childcare work increased during those years from 28% to 37% (Guppy, Sakumoto, & Wilkes, 2019). Canadian women spent almost two hours per day on childcare in 2015, whereas men reported seventy-two minutes per day. Recent time use studies in the United States indicate that, on an average day, 49% of women but only 19% of men reported doing housework, such as cleaning or laundry, and that 69% of women but only 46% of men reported doing food preparation and cleanup (US Bureau of Labor Statistics, 2018). For US adults living in households with children under six years of age, women spent an average of 2.4 hours per day on household activities, as compared to men's 1.3 hours. One study of parents in fifteen European countries revealed a continuing gap between mothers and fathers in time devoted to childcare, although that gap has shrunk in some countries where parental leave policies are in place (Moreno-Colom, 2017). Men in countries or cultures with more egalitarian gender-role attitudes and men with more education spend more time on domestic work (Kan & Laurie, 2016). However, parenthood makes a difference. Across countries, couples with children are less likely to share household work than are couples without children; however, the impact of children appears to be greater in countries with more gender equality (DeRose et al., 2019).

Motherhood is a central to identity for many women (e.g., Wilson, 2007). A woman without children may be seen as (and may feel like) a failure – perhaps not even a real woman (Batool & de Visser, 2016; Bimha & Chadwick, 2016). However, simply producing children is not enough to succeed at this role. Mothers face high standards for their feelings and expectations toward their children (e.g., Kerrick & Henry, 2017). In many Western cultures, motherhood involves aspiring to very high standards of love, self-sacrifice, and taking primary responsibility for children (e.g., Power et al., 2011; Wilson, 2007). Women may feel pressured to conform to an ideology of "intensive mothering" that is child-centered, labor-intensive, emotionally absorbing, and puts the child's needs before the mother's (Ennis, 2014; Hays, 1996). Mothers in various cultures feel the pressure of this ideal and are criticized for failure to meet it (e.g., Aono & Kashiwagi, 2011; Berhane et al., 2018; Cairns, Johnston, & MacKendrick, 2013; Elliott & Bowen, 2018; Shloim et al., 2015). Indeed, the experience of maternal guilt for not living up to cultural ideals of motherhood appears to transcend national boundaries and even, to some extent, public policy differences (Collins, 2020). The expectations surrounding motherhood fit into a broader ideology that women are supposed to nurture and care for others – that they must be sensitive and responsive to the needs of others, even when they themselves are exhausted, stressed, or ill (Forssén et al., 2005; Martinez-Marcos & De la Cuesta-Benjumea, 2014). Unsurprisingly, motherhood is harder on women who have restricted access to resources and/or who face discrimination based on race, ethnicity, or class. For example, in Canada, First Nations women are 20 percent more likely than are White Caucasian women to experience distress and depressive symptoms postpartum (Dharma et al., 2019).

Within the framework of an ideology of caring, motherhood does not appear to be a particularly powerful role. Indeed, this ideology encourages mothers to put their own needs last and to arrange their lives around the needs of their families. Expectations differ across cultures, however. For example, in Japan, women have traditionally been under strong pressure to be mothers, and the mother role has traditionally involved, not only dedication and sacrifice, but also independence and status. Mothers have significant control over family decisions related to their children and they have respected status as an influence group when speaking to government officials about children's needs. Japanese women who have chosen motherhood report having a strong commitment to gaining status, respect, and self-worth from their roles as mothers (Bankart, 1989; Holloway et al., 2006). In matrilineal cultures, as in some Igbo communities in Africa, family lineage is determined through the mother, making mothers a central force in defining their families (Nzegwu, 2004). In other traditionally matrilineal cultures, such as the Tlingit people of North America, women's influence and leadership across all areas of society is acknowledged (Fleek, 2000). It is the mother role that brings community power and prestige to many African women (Sudarkasa, 2004). In some West African cultures, female elders develop the status of "public" mothers to their communities, with authority based upon the symbolism of motherhood (Semley, 2012). African female activists have asserted that their public activism is an extension of their private maternal responsibilities (Healy-Clancy, 2017). Indeed female political leaders in Africa, from Winnie Mandela to Ellen Johnson Sirleaf, have sometimes underlined their legitimacy as leaders by accepting the mantle of "mothers" of their countries. Motherhood has also conferred moral authority on female activists, such as the Mothers of the Plaza de Mayo in Argentina, the Saturday Mothers and the Peace Mothers in Turkey and in Sierra Leone, and the Mothers of the Movement and the Wall of Moms in the United States. These women derive their authority from having lost, or fear of losing, children through violence, war, or persecution, (e.g., Karaman, 2016; Kurtzleben, 2020; Sebastian, 2016).

For sexual minority women, claiming and adapting a motherhood identity may be especially complex. Feeling comfortable as a new mother may depend on a lesbian woman's legal rights and on the degree to which she is "out" at work and in her community (Hennekam & Ladge, 2017; Kasai & Rooney, 2012). In many countries, legal and social recognition of lesbian motherhood is problematic, leading to tension between discretion and visibility, conformity and marginality (e.g., Arita, 2006; Soboćan, 2011; Zhabenko, 2019). On the other hand, some lesbian mothers value the opportunity to create their own mothering roles, in the absence of established traditional roles for lesbian mothers (Hayman & Wilkes, 2017). Lesbian mothers report concerns about discrimination against their children, and may engage in political activism to increase public acceptance of diversity and thus make the world safer for their children (Gartrell et al., 2000). For transgender parents, who do not fit neatly into the female/mother and male/ father model of parental identity, the designation of "mother" may be multidimensional, nonbinary, and fluid – influenced by the degree of acceptance in the public environment, cultural pressures, and relationships with children and partners (Petit, Julien, & Chamberland, 2017, 2018).

The caregiving work that mothers do is not simply mother-to-child physical and emotional support and nurturing. It is also mental, organizational, and goal oriented. Mothers of young children report that they are the primary mental laborers in their families, and that this labor involves such activities as planning, managing, monitoring, and anticipating family needs, remembering what needs to be done, delegating, and instructing (Robertson et al., 2019). This often-invisible work, for which mothers are disproportionately responsible, may strain their well-being and spousal relationships (Ciciolla & Luthar, 2019).

Despite the stereotype that motherhood presumes, and naturally evokes, caring and attachment, there are numerous examples of mothers abandoning (Mueller & Sherr, 2009; Razali et al., 2014) or killing (Tanaka, 2017) their babies, often because of shame, fear of rejection or social stigma, fear of violence, or economic desperation. In cultures, such as parts of China and India, where girls and women are not valued, mothers have historically neglected, abandoned, or killed unwanted female infants (e.g., Miller, 1997). Indeed, historical evidence suggests that this practice was common in all parts of the world (Newman, 2017). In poor societies, with extremely high infant mortality, mothers may refrain from attachment to infants until they have survived their first months of life, sometimes not even naming them. In one desperately poor Brazilian shantytown, mothers had, on average, suffered the death over half of the babies born to them within the first year of life. These mothers favored infants that appeared to have the best chance of survival. They expressed pity toward, but selectively neglected, infants not expected to sur-vive – saying that it was best to let weak children die because they would never be strong enough to defend themselves as adults. Yet, these mothers were very affectionate toward their children and, in the few cases where neglected children survived, the mothers accepted and loved them (Scheper-Hughes, 1985; 1992). In the dismal conditions of this impoverished community, the mothers had only the choice to emphasize grief or resignation when faced with the imminent loss of a sickly child. Their focus on bonding with the stronger infants probably increased the life chances of those infants. Their situation is a reminder that the mother–child bond should be understood in the context of culture and available resources.

Across cultures, then, nurturing and caregiving are defined as women's work, and women often must arrange their lives around bearing children, caring for them, and balancing other responsibilities with the motherhood role. However, women often do not have access to the resources needed to support their children as successfully as they and their communities would like. Although motherhood may be highly regarded, most women cannot choose to focus only on the unpaid work of rearing children; the typical woman in most countries combines motherhood with economic activity outside the home.

## 6 Economic Participation and Power

Cultural expectations and practical issues affect whether women work outside the home. For example, in Yemen, only 6% of women are in the labor force, compared with 21.2% in Afghanistan, 50.3% in Argentina, 61% Australia, and 81% in Bermuda (World Bank, 2020). In the United States, more than 57% of women are in the workforce (World Bank, 2020), and women are 64.3% of primary or co-breadwinners for families (Glynn, 2019). Globally, about 55% of women participate in the paid labor force (World Economic Forum 2019). One factor that depresses women's participation in the labor force is their disproportionate responsibility for unpaid domestic work. The worldwide norm is for women to carry the double burden of both work outside and in the home; around the world, women still do, on average, at least twice as much unpaid work as men do (World Economic Forum, 2019). The size of the gender gap in unpaid work (housework, shopping, care of household members, etc.) varies considerably by country. For example, in Denmark, men report spending about 58 minutes less per day than women do in such activities; in Poland, men spend about 136 fewer minutes performing unpaid work than women do, and in Japan the time difference between women's and men's unpaid work is about 183 minutes (Organization for Economic Co-operation and Development, 2020).

Despite legal prohibitions against sex discrimination in many countries (and a United Nations *Convention on the Elimination of Discrimination against Women* endorsed by most nations), there is ample evidence that women face employment discrimination in hiring, evaluation, advancement, pay, and working conditions – particularly in work settings or occupations that are traditionally male dominated. Women may encounter hostility or deprecation if they are regarded as not fitting into occupational roles because they are violating femininity norms and/or invading masculine turf (Heilman & Caleo, 2018). Additionally, their capabilities may be undervalued and the importance and difficulty of their work diminished simply because they are women (Levanon, England, & Allison, 2009). Finally, international data suggests that people may rationalize discrimination via the notion that women's employment threatens children and family life (Verniers & Vala, 2018). Very public and striking examples of sex discrimination are evident around the world. In the United States, the World Cup champion women's soccer team sued its Federation for pay and working conditions equal to that of the much less successful men's team (Cater, 2020). In Afghanistan, female graduates of the police academy face nonstop harassment, abuse, and threats when they take up their jobs in the security forces, where they make up less than 3 percent of employees (Mashal, 2020). In Japan, one of the nation's premier medical schools admitted that, for at least a decade, it had been systematically rigging its entrance exam by lowering women's scores and giving bonus points to men (Chang, 2018). Such examples have caused outrage, but much discrimination is more subtle. It may feature quietly overlooking the contributions of female employees or providing more challenging and rewarding opportunities to male employees. Research shows, however, that subtle discrimination and bias against women in the workplace can have equally negative consequences as can more blatant discrimination (Jones et al., 2016). Such consequences include adverse effects in terms of individual career (e.g., rank, pay, job stress), organizational commitment (e.g., turnover intentions, performance), physical health (e.g., substance use, cardiovascular health), and psychological health (e.g., self-esteem, depression, life satisfaction).

According to the World Economic Forum (2019), the global gender gap in economic participation and opportunity has closed by only 58 percent to date;

men's average income from all sources (wages, investments, corporate profits, etc.) represents a purchasing power of about $21,000, whereas women's is about $11,000. Worldwide, women are paid less for their work than men are, and the size of the gap is influenced by cultural norms and public policy (Lips, 2018). The global wage gap between men and women stands at about 13.5 percent, and is closing extremely slowly. The World Economic Forum estimates that, at the current rate, it will take 257 years to close the gender gap in economic participation and opportunity. In 2019, women in Burundi actually earned more than men did; however, the earned income of women in most other countries fell well below that of men. Rwanda, Iceland, and Finland had some of the smallest, but still very significant, gender earnings gaps: women's earned income was 72%, 73%, and 72% of men's, respectively (World Economic Forum, 2019). The same data source puts US women's earned income at 66% of men's. The report shows that many countries have far wider income gaps (e.g., in Pakistan, women's earned income was 18% of men's; in Saudi Arabia, women's earned income was 24% of men's).

Depending on the indicators used, the gender wage gap may appear smaller or larger. For example, focusing only on full-time year-round workers, the US Census Bureau (2019) reports that, averaged across all jobs, women earn just over 81.3% of men's median wages. This overall statistic obscures some important differences among women: among full-time year-round US workers, Black women earn 61.7% and Hispanic women earn just 53.9% of what White non-Hispanic men earn. Regardless of the measure used, the region studied, or the race/ethnicity of the sample, however, there is consistently a gap in favor of men. This pay gap, cumulated over a lifetime of employment, translates into a greater likelihood of poverty for women, particularly in old age, since lower wages result in lower pensions and less savings. The average old age poverty rates for women and men in the OECD countries are 15.7% and 10.3% respectively (Organization for Economic Cooperation and Development, 2019).

A wage penalty associated with motherhood, often labeled the "motherhood penalty" contributes significantly to the gender wage gap. Around the world, mothers earn less than both childless women and men do; the gap increases with the number of children a woman has (Grimshaw & Rubery, 2015). For mothers in the United States, the penalty is estimated to be between 2% and 6% per child (Linde Leonard & Stanley, 2020). The wage penalty associated with having children in OECD countries has been found to average 14%, with the highest gaps in Japan and Korea, and the lowest in Italy and Spain (Organization for Economic Co-operation and Development, 2012). Even in Denmark, a country that provides more support than most for mothers, much of the gender gap in earnings is linked to the presence of children (Kleven, Landais, & Søgaard, 2019). In China, researchers have found that the gap increases by about 12% in hourly wages for each additional child, and that it is largest among women living with their husbands' parents and smallest among those living with their own parents (Yu & Xie, 2018). Despite the increase in women's labor force participation over the years, the motherhood penalty does not appear to have shrunk – at least not in the United States (Glauber, 2019).

The penalty stems, in part, from the necessity for mothers to work fewer paid hours to accommodate family responsibilities (and so to have less work experience, job tenure, and opportunities for advancement or mobility), and to accept low-paying jobs based on factors such as flexibility and location, that mesh with childcare responsibilities (Grimshaw & Rubery, 2015). Almost two-thirds of employed women with children in the United States worked full-time in 2018 (Christnacht & Sullivan, 2020). Nonetheless, in part because of the demands of motherhood, women are far more likely than men to work part-time, often in low-paying service and caretaking jobs. However, motherhood penalties are largest for women in high-skill, high-wage positions (England et al., 2016) and for those in female-dominated occupations, even when working full time (Glauber, 2012).

Mothers also face particular stereotyping and discrimination in employment. Pregnant women workers often feel that they are being pushed out of their organizations through lack of career encouragement (Paustian-Underdahl et al., 2019). Mothers, more than childless women, are stereotyped as lacking in competence, job commitment, and availability; are chosen less often for management positions and promotions; and are offered lower starting salaries (Correll, Benard, & Paik, 2007; Cuddy, Fiske, & Glick, 2004; Cunningham & Macan, 2007). Because most cultures do not place primary childcare responsibilities on men, fathers do not face the same discrimination. In fact, in the United States and Canada, fathers are often preferred as employees over men without children (Cuddy et al., 2004) and paid more than childless men if they are married, living with their families, and high-skilled (Cooke & Fuller, 2018; Hodges & Budig, 2010; Killewald, 2013). Even when mothers indisputably prove their competence and commitment, they may still face discrimination, being viewed, especially by female evaluators, as less warm and likable and more hostile than similar workers who are not mothers (Benard & Correll, 2010).

Mothers who clearly signal their devotion to work can sometimes escape the motherhood penalty, at least at the hiring stage (Aranda & Glick, 2014); mothers who work in job contexts where requirements and skills are viewed as congruent with feminine and/or maternal qualities may also evade discrimination based on motherhood (Glass & Fodor, 2018).

The level of pressure for women to take on the greatest share of domestic and childcare responsibilities was laid bare around the world during the stay-at–home orders caused by the global COVID-19 pandemic. The necessity to home-school children and to work remotely, along with financial stress and fear of the illness, has produced psychological distress in parents, especially mothers (Fontanesi et al., 2020; Lauri Korajlija & Jokic-Begic, 2020). In practical terms, the situation has increased the burden on mothers, who often take on the role of primary education providers for their children along with the bulk of domestic work and their paid employment (Burk, Pechenik Mausolf, & Oakleaf, 2020). Among married heterosexual couples in the United States, during the early months of the COVID-19 outbreak, mothers of young children reduced their paid work hours four to five times more than fathers did – even among couples where both members were able to work remotely from home (Collins et al., 2020). An increased gender gap in work hours may disadvantage women in terms of workplace success, and may lead to a higher likelihood of job loss. Arguably, the long-term effect of the pandemic may be to reinforce an ideal of motherhood that places individual responsibility on mothers for childrearing and for handling family and employment responsibilities without structural help (Güney-Frahm, 2020). The changes in gendered distribution of domestic labor, apparently wrought so rapidly by the pandemic, indicate the powerful impact of cultural change on gender roles.

On average, men work in higher-paying and higher-status occupations than women. Such jobs often require a level of energy and time commitments that can be especially challenging for women with childcare responsibilities that are not equally shared by men – especially when (as is usually the case) there is no structural support for families. It is sometimes argued that women earn less than men do because, when choosing employment, they prioritize flexible working arrangements over pay. Ironically, however, if mothers avoid high-power jobs in order to safeguard their flexibility to meet family responsibilities, they may be disappointed. Lower-status and female-dominated jobs often offer the least flexibility to their workers as well as the least pay (Dodson, 2013; Glauber, 2012; Magnusson, 2019). Flexible working arrangements appear more likely to ameliorate gendered pay disadvantages faced by university-educated women in higher-status jobs, and less likely to offer the same result to women in lower-wage occupations (Fuller & Hirsch, 2019). Furthermore, mothers who work in low-wage jobs may be stereotyped as irresponsible when family–work conflicts push them to request flexibility to care for children (Dodson, 2013).

The childcare duties disproportionately assigned to women contribute to occupational segregation and the gendering of power and influence around the world. In most countries, women fill only between 14% and 30% of senior roles in the labor force (World Economic Forum, 2019). Globally, women hold only 12% of positions in cloud computing and 15% of positions in engineering occupations – cutting-edge professions that are linked to high pay, potential growth, and opportunity (World Economic Forum, 2019). In only three countries (Nicaragua, Rwanda, and Costa Rica) are at least 50% of government ministerial positions held by women. In many other countries, the proportion of such powerful positions held by women is abysmally low. For example, women hold 6.5% of such position in the Republic of Iran, 5.3% in Japan, and 3.4% in Lebanon. The same source notes that, in many countries, women hold few positions as legislators, senior officials, or managers. Whereas, for instance, women in Canada and Botswana, respectively hold 35.5% and 38.6% of such influential positions, women hold only 4.9% of these positions in Pakistan, 16.8% in China, and 27% in Italy.

Worldwide, providing childcare resources for employed mothers predicts more workforce participation by mothers (del Mar Alonso-Almeida, 2014) and smaller motherhood wage penalties (Budig, Misra, & Boeckmann, 2016). Countries with policies that encourage the sharing of childcare responsibility between women and men tend to have a more equal balance of men and women in high-paying jobs, and a narrower gender wage gap. In Norway, for example, with the birth of a child, both men and women are entitled to paid parental leave (thirty-five to forty-six weeks for mothers, up to ten weeks for fathers). A government social insurance fund pays parents on leave 80 to 100% of their wages. In Iceland, parents are entitled to shared parental leave of nine months at 80% of salary, and the first six months are divided equally between the two parents. Parents are entitled to this leave regardless of their employment status; unemployed parents receive monthly government grants (Chzhen, Gromada, & Rees, 2019; Weller, 2014). Yemen, on the other hand, mandates shorter paid maternity leave (approximately seventy days), paid for by employers, and no paternity leave. Switzerland provides eight weeks of maternity leave and no paternity leave. These very different leave benefits for new parents likely have a profound influence on women's chances of success in the labor force. Indeed Norway and Iceland have more women in legislative and managerial positions, and narrower gender wage gaps than do Yemen and Switzerland, and Iceland has one of the world's highest labor force participation rates for women (World Economic Forum, 2020). Other variables, such as economic development, factor into national differences in women's workforce success, however. The United States, the only country with no national policy at all to provide paid parental leave, indeed has lower workforce participation rates by women and a larger wage gap than Norway, Iceland, or Switzerland (which all provide at least some support for parents). However, it also has higher workforce participation by women and a narrower wage gap than does Yemen, despite Yemen's provision of maternal leave (World Economic Forum, 2019). It is also worthy of note that formal laws and policies do not always translate into actual support for large numbers of employed women. In India, for instance, a 2017 law mandates twenty-six weeks of paid maternity leave – one of the longest in the world. However, the law applies only to companies with at least ten employees, while about 84% of employed women work in companies with smaller payrolls. Thus, this legislation benefits only a small fraction of employed women (Rajagopalan & Tabarrok, 2019).

A potentially important consideration is that generous leave policies can sometimes backfire: mothers who take even a short break from employment may be perceived as lower in their work commitment or agency and/or may miss opportunities for challenging work assignments that lead to advancement – and may thus end up with lower earnings (Hideg et al., 2018; Livingston, 2013). Particularly for women who work in settings where sex discriminatory attitudes are prevalent, taking advantage of provisions such as family leave may lessen their status as valued employees (Jang, Zippay, & Park, 2016). Indeed, one study suggests that new mothers in the workplace are in a no-win situation: if they take maternity leave, they are seen as less competent and less worthy of organizational rewards; if they do not, they are seen as worse parents and less desirable partners (Morgenroth & Heilman, 2017). However, fathers may sometimes also suffer depression in their earnings and in their reputation as good employees if they modify their employment to accommodate family responsibilities (Coltrane et al., 2013; Harvey & Tremblay, 2018)). Fathers in Germany, for example, suffer wage penalties if they work part-time; however, they do not seem to be penalized for taking parental leave (Bünning, 2016). In Japan, perceived stigmatization and fear of negative evaluation has historically kept the number of men taking paternity leave at a low level, even among men with positive attitudes toward such leave (Miyajima & Yamaguchi, 2017).

In international contexts, the availability of paid maternity leave predicts improved outcomes for both mothers and infants. In the United States, paid maternity leave is associated with lower odds of re-hospitalization for both mothers and infants, along with higher odds of success with exercise and stress management (Jou et al., 2018). Because of the positive impact of maternity protection and the desire to promote gender equality in employment, the International Labour Organization (2020) recommends that all countries provide at least fourteen weeks of maternity leave at a pay level of at least two-thirds of previous earnings, paid for by public funds or social insurance. This standard is far from universally met, particularly for women who work in small businesses, in the informal economy, or in contexts where legal requirements for such leave are not enforced.

The data are clear that, around the world, women face discrimination and restrictions with respect to economic participation. The specifics and degree of such restrictions differ across countries and cultures, but nowhere do women and men experience an even playing field with respect to paid work. The disadvantages that impede women's economic participation connect to women's lack of access, relative to men, to positions of public power and status as well as to wealth. Because they limit women's access to economic resources, they also contribute to women's vulnerability to violence, as shown in the following section.

## 7 Violence

Globally, men are far more likely than women are to be the targets of violence perpetrated by other men, perhaps because many cultures stress a competitive, aggressive ideal of masculinity (Eibach, 2016). However, women are the most frequent targets of male-perpetrated intimate partner and sexual violence. Both intimate partner violence and sexual violence often take place behind closed doors and go unreported by shamed and frightened victims. This under-reporting makes it difficult to obtain accurate estimates.

Intimate partner violence against women is common worldwide. According to one review of 134 studies, with data drawn from six continents, lifetime physical violence rates ranged from 10.6 to 78.7% of women, lifetime emotional violence ranged from 7.4 to 92.0%, and lifetime sexual violence ranged from 3.4 to 58.6% – findings which led the authors to conclude that violence against women is at epic proportions in many societies (Alhabib, Nur, & Jones, 2010). Another study that examined data from eighty-one countries revealed that, globally, 27.8% to 32.2% of women aged fifteen and over had experienced physical and/or sexual intimate partner violence during their lifetime (Devries et al., 2013). Still another international study indicated that, globally, more than one-third of female homicides are committed by an intimate partner (Stöckl et al., 2013). In one review of research on the rates of non-partner sexualized violence against women, 7.2% of women worldwide reported experiencing non-partner sexualized violence in their lifetime. Rates varied by country, with the highest rates seen in the central part of sub-Saharan Africa (21.0%) and the lowest rates in South Asia (3.3%) – although the authors note the difficulty of making cross-national comparisons because of differences in the availability and quality of data (Abrahams et al., 2014). Experience of intimate partner violence may be particularly common among women with vulnerabilities that increase their dependence on a partner, such as physical disability, mental illness, marginalized social status, and low access to economic resources (Barbosa et al., 2019; Barnawi, 2017; Cases et al., 2014; Niu & Laidler, 2015). Refugee and migrant women, in particular – a group that often has few protections – are at high risk for sexualized and intimate partner violence (Ferris, 2007; Gonçalves & Matos, 2016; Hynes & Cardozo, 2000; Keygnaert, Vettenburg, & Temmerman, 2012; Voolma, 2018). Within countries, racial and ethnic minority women are disproportionately likely to be affected by intimate partner violence (e.g., Black et al., 2011; Vives-Cases et al., 2014). For example, in Canada, Indigenous women are more than seven times more likely than non-Indigenous women to be murdered (O'Donnell & Wallace, 2011). The rates of violence against aboriginal women in Canada have been deemed by a government inquiry to be so frequent as to amount to genocide (Kennedy, 2019).

Violence against women is likely to involve repeated patterns of abusive activity over time rather than isolated incidents and is frequently perpetrated by men (spouses, relatives, acquaintances) who are known to the victims. Researchers in the West have identified different types of intimate partner violence that vary in severity and mutuality between partners (Johnson, 1995; 2008). The most severe, termed "intimate terrorism," is usually one-sided, male-to female, coercive, and escalates over time. By contrast, "common couple violence" is mutual between partners, less severe and coercive, and does not tend to escalate. A third type, "violent resistance," is performed by victims of intimate terrorism in response to their partners' violence, and a rarer fourth type, "mutual violent control," involves both partners in mild to moderate levels of violence against the other. In Western countries, studies of these different types of intimate partner violence reveal that, although men do experience violence from their female partners, women are more likely than men are to be targets of severe violence from intimate partners. However, more research is needed to understand how the role of culture, particularly along dimensions of gender equality, relates to the prevalence and consequences of interpersonal violence (Williams, McKelvey, & Frieze, 2014).

Whatever the pattern and whatever the country, there is some tendency to blame female victims for causing the violence, and women may experience difficulties getting justice in the criminal justice system (Ferrer-Pérez & Bosch-Fiol, 2014; Ivert, Merlo, & Gracia, 2018; Koss, White, & Lopez, 2017; Watts & Zimmerman, 2002). Cultural attitudes that grant higher status, power, and resources to men and that tolerate or legitimate intimate partner violence against women support these patterns (Gracia, Lila, & Santirso, 2020). The notion that men should be the heads of their households implies that they should be able to control "their" women, and women's dependence on men for economic and social resources can mean they have few options for leaving an abusive situation. For example, a study of Kosovo women physically abused by male partners indicated that a patriarchal culture and strictly defined gender roles, along with poverty and a lack of support left these women particularly vulnerable to domestic violence (Kelmendi, 2015). Interviews with men in Vietnam suggest that cultural definitions and norms of masculinity incorporate intimate partner violence as a way of responding to threats to men's status (James-Hawkins et al., 2019). Research with a sample of young men in Bangladesh has indicated that community-level gender norms were significantly related to married men's coercive behavior with their partners: more gender-equitable norms were negatively linked to men's use of controlling behavior (James-Hawkins et al., 2018). An investigation of women's risk for intimate partner violence in Nepal suggests that community social norms with respect to acceptance of partner violence are important predictors of that risk (Clark, Ferguson et al., 2018). Anthropological research has found that cultures that emphasize male dominance, separate spheres for women and men, and high levels of interpersonal violence have a higher incidence of rape (Sanday, 1981; 2003).

A number of societal and community characteristics and conditions are associated with higher levels of intimate partner violence. For example, during the COVID-19 crisis of 2020, when movement restrictions were imposed in most countries to stop the spread of the virus, the necessity for women to stay at home in isolation with their partners apparently contributed to a worldwide rise in intimate partner violence (Taub, 2020). In general, communities that are high in concentrated economic disadvantage and low in social cohesion also tend to be high in intimate partner violence; however, some socioeconomic variables, such as levels of education in a community, are inconsistently related to intimate partner violence. Communities in which there is a high degree of acceptance by women that a husband may beat his wife under certain circumstances also tend to have higher levels of intimate partner violence (VanderEnde et al., 2012). Women are less likely to experience violence in countries where there are legal strictures against intimate partner violence (Kovacs, 2018). Religion makes a difference too: women living in majority Christian countries appear more likely than are women in majority Muslim countries to experience intimate partner violence (Kovacs, 2018). Again, cross-national comparisons may be problematic because of national and cultural differences in reporting.

On an individual level, men's attitudes toward women and violence are significant predictors of their perpetration of sexual assault (McDermott et al., 2015). US men high in hostile masculinity and male dominance beliefs are more likely than are other men to self-report past sexual aggression (Murnen, Wright, & Kaluzny, 2002). Among both US and Chinese university students, gender-role attitudes are important predictors of attitudes toward intimate partner violence (Lin et al., 2016). In one US sample of men aged twenty-one to thrity-five, those who scored high on adherence to anti-feminine norms and on the tendency to experience stress when in subordinate positions to women were most likely to have reported sexual aggression toward an intimate partner in the past year (Smith et al., 2015). Among Korean male university students, patriarchal sex-role attitudes (beliefs that men should have more power and authority to control women and to exert violence when their partner does not cooperate) directly predict the perpetration of dating violence, and also have an indirect effect on perpetration via acceptance of dating violence (You & Shin, 2020). Threats to certain aspects of masculine gender norms may promote male violence against women. For example, men who believe they should experience power and control may try to exert that control over a spouse when control is denied elsewhere, and men who accept that violence is an appropriately manly way to solve disputes may rely on violence to gain compliance from their partners (Williams, McKelvey, & Frieze, 2014). Women who report intimate partner violence are more likely than are other women to be surrounded by men who engage in controlling and limiting behavior toward them (Ellsberg et al., 2008).

Advances in technology have expanded the ways in which women and girls can be targeted, through various forms of cyberviolence – a broad category that includes cyberbullying, online harassment, cyberstalking, nonconsensual pornography (NCP), and cyber dating abuse (Backe, Lilleston, & McCleary-Sills, 2018). Little research addresses this issue in low- and middle-income countries. However, one survey of adults in twenty-eight countries found that, globally, 17% said that their own child had experienced cyberbullying. Across countries, between 1% and 37% of parents reported that their children had been victims of cyberbullying, with parents in India, Brazil, and the United States reporting the highest percentages, and parents in Russia, Japan, and Chile reporting the lowest percentages (Ipsos.com, 2018). Women and girls are somewhat more likely than men and boys to be victims of cyberbullying, although the proportions may depend on the context (e.g., social media vs. video games) (Livingstone et al., 2011; Wang et al., 2019). Unlike face-to-face stalking, where most stalkers are former partners, cyber harassers are more likely to be complete strangers or casual acquaintances. Technology has also led to an increase in NCP, or the posting of nude or sexually graphic images of another individual without their consent (Eaton, Jacobs, & Ruvalcaba, 2017; Johansen, Pedersen, & Tjørnhøj-Thomsen, 2019). Laws that have not kept pace with the increase in social media use, lack of training for police officers, and jurisdiction issues can make it difficult for victims to prevent and stop cyberviolence.

## 7.1 Violence against Women to Enact the Gender Hierarchy

In certain situations, violence against women serves as a public performance of gender hierarchy, male status, and masculinity: an overt statement about men's ownership of, control over, and right to authority over "their" women. One tragic example is honor killing: the murder of a woman whose behavior is deemed to have brought dishonor to her husband, father, and/or other family members (Van Osch et al., 2013). However, in broad terms, a similar analysis can be applied to situations where any husband insults, berates, humiliates, or hits his wife in public, or where any man who claims authority over a female relative publicly exerts coercive control over her. The man's public assertion of dominance over a spouse or daughter may occur in reaction to behavior he interprets as insubordinate – as threatening to his role as acknowledged head of the family. The behavior that prompts honor killing specifically usually involves women transgressing cultural boundaries of propriety, chastity and/or fidelity in ways that may range from dressing in unapproved ways, going unchaperoned to particular places, or being in the company of unrelated men, to having intimate relationships outside of marriage, being raped, or even marrying a man without family approval. In cultures with a strong orientation toward honor, a woman's lack of sexual purity is deemed to bring dishonor to the man and to his whole family (Cihangir, 2013); a man's reputation and honor can be restored through banishment or killing of the offending woman. Honor killings, most often carried out by a male relative, have been estimated to claim the lives of more than 5,000 women every year world-wide. This estimate is likely too low, given that such killings may be unreported or disguised as suicides or missing persons (Caffaro, Ferraris, & Schmidt, 2014; Chesler, 2010). They occur all over the world and often receive lenient treatment by legal systems (Chesler, 2010). One investigation of honor killings in Pakistan found 1,957 such homicides between 2004 and 2007 (Nasrullah, Haqqi, & Cummings, 2009). These authors reported that most of the victims were adult married women, that alleged extramarital affairs were the most frequent reason for the killing, and that the perpetrators were most often husbands or brothers.

In communities where cultural masculinity norms tie a man's honor and standing in the community to his ability to control his wife and daughters, a man may feel that his most important possession is his honor. An indiscreet woman is seen as bringing shame on her family and destroying that one important possession – a possession that is ultimately viewed as much more important than the woman herself. The cultural assignment of higher value to men's honor and community standing than to women's lives is a grim indicator that women's welfare is considered inconsequential relative to men's.

Ironically, rape can serve as a punishment, visited on women for violating rules of sexual propriety, or even simply for intruding into spaces, occupations, or situations where they "do not belong." Rape also enacts male–male aggression: one man can dishonor another by raping his wife, daughter, sister, or mother. The rape of women during war by enemy soldiers is a common way of harming women while also dishonoring and demoralizing a whole community, leaving a lasting legacy of humiliation and bitterness (Holt, 2013). For example, during the war in Bosnia in the early 1990s, an estimated 20,000 to 50,000 women were raped (Turton, 2017); during the 1994 Rwandan genocide, between one-quarter and one-half million women were raped (Human Rights Watch, 1996). In 2014, thousands of Yazidi women in Iraq were kidnapped and enslaved by ISIS fighters, raped and beaten repeatedly, and often forced to bear children. Such violence often takes place within a cultural context that is deeply patriarchal, so that women are ashamed to discuss it and others in their communities hold the women as somehow responsible for their own victimization (Holt, 2013). In the case of the Yazidi women, the children that resulted from their rapes were later rejected by their communities after the women were rescued. These women, already traumatized, were forced to give up their children in order to be accepted back into their families and communities (Arraf, 2020).

## 7.2 The Business of Violence against Women

The abuse of women is often a for-profit enterprise. Sexual exploitation of girls and women, trafficking of women for the purpose of prostitution or forced labor, pornography that exploits images of female humiliation – all are thriving businesses that span the globe. The United Nations reports that, among the many thousands of persons who are trafficked across national borders each year into situations of sexual exploitation and/or forced servitude, some 72 percent are women (49 percent) and girls (23 percent) (United Nations Office on Drugs and Crime, 2018). Refugee women and women who live in conflict areas are particularly vulnerable to trafficking due to lack of safe shelter, economic opportunities, and survival options; desperate social conditions; discrimination due to gender, ethnicity, race, or religion; the erosion of rule of law and/or weak governments in conflict or crisis areas; and the targeting of refugee camps by criminals. Like other forms of violence against women, trafficking is grounded in cultural norms and practices that provide men with more access to resources and in attitudes that support male control over women and the primacy of male needs and wants over women's welfare. Despite ongoing attempts by international nongovernmental organizations to stem these practices, many governments have responded weakly to the problem.

## 7.3 Impact of Violence on Women's Health and Well-Being

International studies have found that women who have experienced partner violence in their lifetimes are more likely than other women to report poor health, including difficulty walking, trouble carrying out daily activities, pain, memory loss, dizziness, vaginal discharge, emotional distress, suicidal thoughts, and suicide attempts (Devries et al., 2011; Ellsberg et al., 2008). In low-income countries, gender-based violence against women and girls is linked to sexually transmitted disease, unplanned pregnancy, and abortion (Grose et al., 2020). A mountain of evidence indicates that the experience of intimate partner violence predicts psychological stress (Yim & Kofman, 2019).

The psychological impact of violence can be profound, and has implications not only for individual women's mental health, but also for the ability of women as a group to thrive and to achieve success, status, and power relative to men. Research in many countries, including Spain (Matud, 2005), El Salvador (Bermúdez, Matud, & Buela-Casal, 2009), and Jordan (Al-Modallal et al., 2012) show that women victimized by partners often experience long-lasting anxiety, depression, stress, and feelings of insecurity, making it more difficult for them to function effectively. Women who remain in a relationship where they are mistreated may label themselves "stupid" – an expression of shame that can contribute to further demoralization (Enander, 2010). Women and girls who live in situations where violence against women is common learn to be alert, careful, vigilant, avoidant, and fearful of further violence (Brown & Gourdine, 2001; Khalid, 1997). The necessity for caution may, in some respects, increase their resourcefulness and coping skills, but it also limits their mobility and interferes with their economic and social opportunities. Thus, an atmosphere of violence against women, whether in the private context of the home or the public context of the street, serves as an effective way of controlling women.

Around the world, then, women experience disproportionate amounts of serious intimate partner violence as well as some other types of violence such as cyberviolence and street harassment. Girls and women are also more subject than boys and men to trafficking. Much violence against women is enabled by cultural norms and structures that privilege men in terms of resources and that support male control over women. Violence against women used to be viewed as a private, interpersonal, family matter. However, international-policy analysts now cite violence against women as both a public health problem and a human rights issue. The shift to viewing anti-female violence as a public policy concern may be a direct result of women's increasing access to resources, such as education, employment, and a voice in the media, that promote their movement into positions of public power and leadership.

## 8 Leadership, Power, and Feminist Activism

Across cultures, men hold more public positions of leadership than do women. For example, the World Economic Forum (2019) reports that, globally, women hold only 25 percent of seats in parliaments and 21 percent of government ministerial positions. Around the world, women are routinely stereotyped as less powerful, dominant, influential, and suited to be leaders and are ascribed lower in status and importance than men (e.g., Fiske, 2017; Glick et al., 2004; Koenig et al., 2011; Smith et al., 2019; Willemsen, 2002). Across cultural groups, gender stereotypes affect respondents' perceptions of leaders; indeed, in one study, male managers from Nordic and Anglo cultural groups (considered the most egalitarian) indicated disparagement of women's performance on the most valued leadership competencies (Prime et al., 2008). Perhaps because of these stereotypes, women's leadership potential is ignored more often than men's (Player et al., 2019). Women themselves feel uncomfortable – as if violating a gendered prohibition on immodesty – when promoting their own strengths (Smith & Huntoon, 2013). Furthermore, respondents indicate a lower likelihood of voting for female politicians who are perceived as seeking power than for female candidates not seen as power-seeking – a pattern that is not found for male politicians (Okimoto & Brescoll, 2010). The association of men with power is so normative that women who behave in overtly powerful ways are often disparaged, even sometimes by other women, as unfeminine, unattractive, and unlikeable (Parks-Stamm, Heilman, & Hearns, 2008; Rudman, Moss-Racusin, Phelan et al., 2012), and penalized via hostility and harassment (Leskinen, Rabelo, & Cortina, 2015). If they persist, they may even be targeted by explicit threats of violence – as in the case of female political candidates in the United States (Astor, 2018), or female members of the British Parliament (Specia, 2019). Indeed, in a survey of women in politics across thirty-nine countries, 44 percent of respondents said they had received threats of death, rape, assault, or abduction (Inter-Parliamentary Union, 2016). Another study of women in politics across eight countries found multiple instances of threats and abuse: a female candidate's house set afire in Sri Lanka, female candidates subjected to verbal and physical abuse in Ghana, murder threats against a female candidate in Lebanon (Westminster Foundation for Democracy, 2018). Negative reactions to powerful women may be prompted, not just by women's violation of gender stereotypic expectations, but also by respondents' negative moral emotions rooted in the motivation to preserve the gender status hierarchy (Brescoll, Okimoto, & Vial, 2018).

Disparagement and underestimation of powerful women is not universal, however. In certain Native American cultures, women have traditionally been ascribed high levels of spiritual and political power (Kehoe, 1995), and women in some Indigenous cultures exercise considerable influence and leadership (Gambrell, 2016). Some cultures make exceptions for older women, whose perceived power may increase with age (Freidman et al., 1992). Among groups such as the Maori and the Lahu, there is a recognition of women's authority, and women may achieve high status as leaders, elders, and wise, powerful matriarchs (Dashu, 1990; Forster, Palmer, & Barnett, 2016). The near-universal stereotype that men are more suited than women are to be leaders and managers has not been found among respondents in Hawaii (de Pillis et al., 2008).

## 8.1 Interpersonal Power

The ability to wield interpersonal influence rests on control of resources: the capacity to reward, punish, or convince others to take an action or position they did not originally intend to take (French & Raven, 1959). These resources vary along a dimension of concrete (money, objective information, physical strength) to personal (expressed disapproval, affection or admiration) and may involve mainly individual relationships or cultural expectations and norms. Since access to such resources tends to be gendered (e.g., men have more money, more physical strength, more status), the exertion of interpersonal power is gendered.

One important, culturally mediated resource is legitimate authority. Where men are deemed to have legitimate authority over women, the full force of cultural norms helps men to wield power over women. If cultural norms dictate that the man is "head of the house," a woman opposing her husband on any decision must push against not just her husband's individual arguments, threats, or promises, but the weight of cultural expectations that a wife should give in to her husband's wishes.

Because, in most cultures, power, dominance, and ambition are deemed unfeminine, both men and women penalize women who exhibit these characteristics – including female workers who are successful in masculine occupations (Rudman, Moss-Racusin, Phelan et al., 2012). The counterintuitive finding that women themselves sometimes penalize powerful, dominant women may be due in part to social comparison. Women who see themselves as possessing these masculine qualities are less likely to penalize powerful women (Lawson & Lips, 2014). To avoid penalization, women who want to exert influence may learn to do so by "softening" their approach and/or their image. Indeed, researchers find that women can defuse potentially negative reactions to their power by emphasizing such qualities as cooperativeness and concern for others (Carli, 2017; Phelan & Rudman, 2010), and by expressing dominance in subtle rather than explicit ways (Williams & Tiedens, 2016).

## 8.2 Public Leadership

Women are underrepresented in positions of public leadership, including not only high-profile political and corporate leadership, but also leadership in grassroots organizations (Kaufman & Grace,. 2011) and entrepreneurial leadership (Harrison, Leitch, & McAdam, 2015). As of this writing, women headed only 19 of 193 national governments (Council on Foreign Relations, 2020). Of these 193 countries, the governments of only 14 had cabinets made up of at least 50 percent women, and only 4 had at least 50 percent women in the national legislature. The Gender Inequality Index (GII), an index conceived by The United Nations Development Program, provides one way to quantify women's public power and compare it across countries. Using this index, which includes measures of women's political participation, workforce participation, education levels, and reproductive health, it is possible to compare countries in terms of gender equality and women's empowerment. Recent statistics show Switzerland, Norway, Sweden, Denmark, and the Netherlands as the countries in which women and men's power was closest to equal in 2018. These countries have index scores lower than 0.05, where 0.0 would indicate gender equality. By contrast, Yemen, Papua New Guinea, and Chad have very high GII scores (greater than 0.70), indicating a great deal of inequality in the distribution of public power between women and men. GII scores for the United States, the United Kingdom, and Canada are 0.182, 0.119, and 0.083 respectively (United Nations Development Program, 2019). Another measure, the Global Gender Gap Index, developed by the World Economic Forum, includes indicators of political empowerment, educational attainment, economic participation and opportunity, and health and survival. In 2020, the countries ranking at the top of this overall index were Iceland, Norway, Finland, Sweden, Nicaragua, and New Zealand. Focusing only on the political empowerment subindex, which comprises measures of the proportions of women in parliament and in minister-ial positions and well as the number of years with a female head of state, reveals the following countries in the top ten: Iceland, Norway, Nicaragua, Rwanda, Finland, Costa Rica, Bangladesh, Spain, Sweden, and South Africa (World Economic Forum, 2019).

What cultural factors promote public leadership by women? One dimension appears to be the degree to which a culture accepts hierarchies and an unequal distribution of power. In one twenty-five-country study, countries with strong acceptance of hierarchies were also characterized by high gender inequality (Glick, 2006). Other contextual issues also appear to be important. Women are most likely to be evaluated harshly as leaders in situations where people are not used to female leaders, settings where most of the participants are male, and leadership positions that seem to call for a directive "masculine" leadership style (Eagly, Makhijani, & Klonsky, 1992). Not surprisingly, cultural settings that feature patriarchal structures, explicit favoring of males over females, and the routine assignment of women to nurturing family roles, provide especially difficult contexts for women to ascend into public leadership roles (Sidani, Konrad, & Karam, 2015). As noted previously, female political leaders have sometimes adjusted to these requirements either by styling themselves as matriarchs or "mothers" of their countries (thus adopting a "feminine" aspect to their leadership role) or by trying to appear tougher than the men (Anuradha, 2008).

The presence of women in visible leadership positions may increase the perceived normalcy of female leadership and thus reduce resistance. It may also help young women to believe in the possibility that they can be leaders – a belief sometimes found to be weaker than men's (Killeen, López-Zafra, & Eagly, 2006; Lips, 2000, 2001; Sheppard, 2018). For example, where village leadership positions in certain randomly selected villages in India were reserved for women, the gender gap in aspirations among both girls and their parents was reduced (Beaman et al., 2012). Thus, cultures in which female leaders are less rare may nurture increased female leadership. Apfelbaum (1993) suggested this conclusion in an early cross-cultural study that revealed large differences in the experiences of female leaders in Norway and France. Norwegian women in leadership roles relished and felt entitled to their power; French women, by contrast, felt isolated, lonely, and continually under siege in their positions. Apfelbaum attributed the difference to cultural context: at the time of the study, Norway was a country where female leadership was common, expected, and supported; French women, by contrast, were trying to lead in a country where female leaders were still an anomaly. Apfelbaum's conclusion gains support from other research indicating that women's experience and construction of leadership is shaped by social and community context. Interviews with female leaders indicate that their approach to leadership is significantly shaped by their upbringing and their early environment, as well as by the availability of supportive networks and alliances (Elliott & Stead, 2008). Female leaders often list family support as critical, and strong professional networks as providing invaluable support and critical advice, "to avoid being ground down by people who have decided that you are not worth anything. Or that you are to be pigeon-holed" (Elliott & Stead, 2008, p. 177). These women's stories suggest that they experience leadership as relational and as embedded in the social and organizational environment. Researchers have also found that, with respect to leadership aspiration, women and men respond differently to interpersonal and collective aspects of a cooperative organizational climate: women's leadership aspirations are more likely than men's to be linked to cooperative interpersonal relationships within an organization (Fritz & Knippenberg, 2017). This is not likely to be because women are inherently more cooperative than men (there is little evidence that this is the case), but rather because they have learned that cooperative relationships are the most effective and least threatening way for them to approach leadership within their organizations.

A study of female managers in Saudi Arabia and the United Kingdom found that the two groups of women had very different notions of networking and mentoring and received different forms of support. Saudi Arabian women linked mentoring and networking with family members, whereas women in the United Kingdom viewed these processes as occurring via workplace or wider professional networks (Abalkhail & Allan, 2015). Many of the Saudi women interviewed for this study cited their fathers or husbands as facilitators and supporters of their careers. They did not have mentors within their organizations, and they did not have access to men's networks except through their male guardians. Women in the United Kingdom, on the other hand, were far more likely to experience either formally structured or informal mentoring within their organizations or their wider professional networks. Women in both countries, however, encountered challenges in seeking out mentoring and supportive networks and faced a longer, more tortuous path to top management than did their male colleagues. Depending on the cultural context, women aspiring to leadership positions must develop varied strategies to resist and negotiate gender discrimination and exclusionary power structures. In Saudi Arabia, for instance, women in leadership roles note that they are hindered by the guardianship system and by patriarchal values that pervade not only their organizations but also the wider society. They argue for an increased role for government in dismantling these systems and the accompanying gender stereotypes, and they use resistance strategies such as deliberately speaking up, voicing concerns, asserting their rights, and asking critical questions in their efforts to overcome discrimination (Abalkhail, 2019).

Women may seek knowledge and expertise in the quest to enhance their influence as leaders. However, expertise can actually backfire on women: some research shows that women are *less* influential and perceived as less expert when they possess expertise – an effect that is reversed for men (Thomas-Hunt & Phillips, 2004). The legitimization of female leadership through explicit cultural rules and laws or by strong and obvious cultural norms may have a positive effect on women's access to such roles. For example, a laboratory study compared the influence over an all-male group of a female leader who either had or had not received special training and was introduced by a male experimenter as either randomly appointed or especially trained to lead the group (Yoder, Schleicher, & McDonald, 1998). Only the women who were both trained and legitimated by the experimenter were effective in influencing their groups' performance. Simply placing women, even expert women, in leadership positions, without legitimizing them through some cultural authority, is not sufficient to ensure their power. Without such legitimization, female power-holders are seen as less deserving of authority than their male counterparts, receive less cooperation and respect, and may struggle to escape a self-reinforcing cycle in which they respond negatively to subordinates' rejection and incur further negativity (Vial, Napier, & Brescoll, 2016).

## 8.3 Collective Power: Feminist Activism

Despite the barriers to claiming power, women working together have found numerous ways to challenge cultural stereotypes and restrictions based on gender. Much of the feminist activism in the service of gender equality around the world has started with small groups of concerned women and has focused on a specific concrete issue. For example, in 1990, forty-seven women drove around Riyadh, the capital of Saudi Arabia, in protest of the nation's longstanding ban against women driving. These women were ultimately arrested, and several lost their jobs, but this act prompted others to protest the ban over the next twenty-seven years. In 2017, the country announced that it would overturn the ban and women would be able to drive starting in June 2018 (Hubbard, 2017). In another example, feminists in New Zealand waged a five-year struggle to obtain pay equity for healthcare workers in residential care settings and home and community support services – workers who are most often ethnic minority and migrant women. Despite an initial stance from the government that pay equity for this group was too expensive, activists used intersecting strategies to argue successfully that equal pay legislation had not achieved its purpose of preventing discriminatory pay for work typically undervalued *because* it is performed by women. This activism eventually led to a negotiated settlement (McGregor & Davies, 2019).

However, feminist activism, like other forms of activism, has also often erupted from a simmering and overarching sense of grievance and gender injustice rather than a single issue. Such was the case, for example, for the 2017 Women's March, which drew huge numbers of people to protests in Washington, DC, and cities around the world (Martin & Smith, 2020). At the time, it was deemed the largest political demonstration in US history, with participants loudly registering their commitment to gender equality and their concern about misogyny, sexism, racism, and heterosexism.

On a more formal level, events such as the World Conferences on Women have been organized to promote the advancement of women worldwide. The Fourth World Conference, hosted in Beijing in 1995, included 189 countries (attracting nearly 50,000 individuals) and produced the *Beijing Declaration and Platform for Action*, which became a touchstone for promoting changes around the world through women's advocacy groups and governments (United Nations, 1997). For example, prompted by the conference, Rwanda adopted a quota system for electing government parliamentary and cabinet seats, requiring 30% of the seats to go to women. In 2020, 61.3% of the members of Rwanda's lower or single House of Parliament were women, up from 17.1% in 1997. Among other countries that adopted quotas, Bolivia and the United Arab Emirates each had at least 50% women in their parliaments in 2020, more than doubling their representation. Globally, the percentage of women in parliaments more than doubled in the twenty-five years following the Beijing conference, from 11.3% to almost 25% (Inter-Parliamentary Union, 2020). These female parliamentarians have provided the driving force behind many legislative changes around the world, including the overturning of gender-discriminatory laws and the passing of legislation aimed at ending domestic violence.

Title IX in the United States illustrates the impact of strong legislation aimed at gender equity. In 1972, inspired and pushed by the leadership of Senator Patsy Mink, the US Congress passed Title IX, which prohibits sex discrimination in any educational institution funded by the federal government. This legislation bars schools from excluding female students from classes, sports, or other activities held within the institution (US Department of Labor, n.d.). Among the many significant changes produced by this legislation, the most dramatic may have been in the realm of athletics. In the first four decades after the passage of Title IX, high school girls' athletic participation increased from fewer than 300,000 to almost 3.3 million, and college women's athletic participation increased from about 30,000 women prior to Title IX to more than 214,000 women (National Coalition for Women & Girls in Education, 2017).

Legislative change does not necessarily originate from concerned legislators, however. External pressure on governments also leads to new laws or to more stringent enforcement of existing laws. After the brutal rape and murder of a woman on a bus in New Delhi, public protests led to the creation of a panel to analyze rape laws in India. Based on the panel's recommendations, the President signed an ordinance that expanded criminal laws on violence against women, making new offenses, such as voyeurism, stalking, trafficking of women, and acid attacks punishable under criminal law (Yardley & Bagri, 2013). Furthermore, activism is important to maintaining existing good legislation. As of this writing, for instance, women in Turkey are rallying against a plan to withdraw their country from the Istanbul Convention, a European convention on combating and preventing violence against women that was signed in 2011 (CNN Wire, 2020).

Feminist activism routinely includes not just legislative strategies, but research, education and training, networking, and providing economic resources for women. For example, digital technology has provided feminists with the opportunity to network with others worldwide in order to communicate, analyze issues, and organize activities to support women. This ease of networking can have complicated effects: both the advantages of creating digital spaces where users can both learn about and take action on certain issues, and the challenges of participating in an online discussion of events, such as sexual assault, that are deeply personal and upsetting (Mendes, Ringrose, & Keller, 2018).

Much like the consciousness-raising groups of early second-wave feminism, sharing stories online can create a sense of solidarity and support and help women to connect their personal experiences to broad structural social problems. However, maintaining these sites and online campaigns can be emotionally taxing for the organizers, and online trolling and abuse is common. Twitter users may engage in "hashtag feminism" by sharing experiences, views, and resources both to promote political actions and to help others who have been victimized by violence or discrimination (Li et al., 2020). Such social media sharing can have a powerful personal and political impact. One study analyzed 3,500 Facebook posts in the *#IAmNotAfraidToSayIt* Facebook campaign started in Ukraine to raise awareness of sexual violence and sexual harassment in that country. These networked conversations, in which people shared their personal stories, appeared to have had a significant impact on the ways people talked and thought about gender-based violence, even beyond the digital sphere. The shared Facebook posts moved the issue out of the realm of shame and silence and into a political discourse that included feminist resistance and feminist critiques of gender roles, discrimination, and violence (Lokot, 2018).

Education to help bring long-accepted anti-woman cultural practices into focus has been a key aspect of feminist activism. In Nigeria, where rape is a serious issue, many rape victims remain silent because they fear physical or social punishment for speaking about the incident (Chiazor et al., 2016). Activist groups work with community leaders to change the norms that compel this silence. They challenge the norms by setting up media interviews and press briefings, distributing information, and using popular theatre to promote awareness of women's rights (Onyejekwe, 2008). In India, individuals perform "street theatre" to promote awareness about women's issues; such performances are also used by South Asian American women to address issues such as sexual violence and immigration rights (Garlough, 2008; 2013). Education on feminist issues such as pressure to conform to destructive cultural standards of beauty, the gender pay gap, discrimination against mothers, and intimate partner violence helps to foreground practices that may be so ingrained in a culture as to be taken for granted and essentially invisible.

In many cultural contexts, then, women are moving gradually into positions of formal power and leadership, dismantling old assumptions that leadership implies masculinity. They are also mobilizing collectively to challenge societal forces that have restricted their power and influence. The shape and the specific goals of women's activism differs across countries and cultures; however, the ease and speed with which information now spreads around the world means that activist movements often draw inspiration and ideas from one another. Movement in the direction of a more gender-balanced distribution of power and leadership appears inexorable; however, the unevenness and relative slowness of the change speaks to the continued pervasiveness of structural and attitudinal barriers to women's leadership.

## 9 Conclusion: Women as Shapers, Keepers, and Prisoners of Cultural Traditions?

Across cultural contexts, women confront many of the same issues: appearance pressures, rules and norms about sexuality, the possibility of pregnancy, societal emphasis on motherhood as a central role for women, intimate partner and sexual violence, discrimination at work, the necessity to perform a delicate dance with respect to leadership, and finding ways to resist denigration, subjugation, and restriction. Common threads through these issues, although enacted in different ways in different contexts, tend to be a gender hierarchy that puts males at the top and a sense, often among both men and women, that males are entitled to be in that position.

The restrictions on and implicit or explicit assignment of lower status to women and girls than to men and boys are woven into many traditional practices and beliefs. This is obvious in certain situations: women's exclusion from certain roles, occupational positions, and places; body-mutilating practices such as foot binding and female genital mutilation or cutting; tolerance for family violence against women. Ironically, it is often women who act as guardians and enforcers of such traditions. For centuries, Chinese mothers performed the painful ritual of foot binding on their daughters. Female genital cutting, which adversely affects the health of millions of girls and women, is usually enforced and carried out by women, in order to protect their daughters and granddaughters from anticipated dishonor and social exclusion (UNICEF, 2013). One study of attitudes toward domestic violence across forty-nine low- and middle-income countries found that, in thirty-six of the countries, women were more likely than men were to say that a husband was justified in beating his wife under certain conditions (Sardinha & Catalán, 2018). However, women's endorsement and enforcement of oppressive gendered traditions tends to occur under the umbrella of patriarchal belief systems that enshrine male dominance, men as the heads of families, and females as subordinate to males. Variations of such belief systems permeate cultures around the world and are more strongly endorsed by men than women (Yoon et al., 2015).

However, even the more benign traditions that label women as the "heart" of the family can also place an undue burden on women. Patriarchal belief systems place the responsibility for caretaking and domestic work squarely on women

(Yoon et al., 2015). The responsibility for maintaining the rhythms of culture – for producing traditional holiday meals and practices, for teaching children the culturally appropriate ways to behave, for maintaining a comfortable and respectable home, for keeping open the lines of communication among family members, are all expectations for women. Indeed, when traditional cultures are under threat, it may fall most strongly on women to act as agents of cultural preservation, to protect cultural legacies and pass them to future generations (e.g., McCloskey, 2007; Popper-Giveon, 2009). Preservation of positive traditions – whether within the family or in the wider culture – is an important task that can contribute to the comfort, security, and well-being of the community. However, the relegation of so much of this responsibility to women may weigh heavily, and may make it difficult for them to explore possibilities and support beneficial changes.

For women whose families have immigrated to a new culture, an emphasis on maintaining traditions from their home culture rather than engaging with the new culture may help to keep them isolated and rob them of opportunities to feel at home in their new country. Some research suggests that, in the process of acculturation, men may increase their adherence to traditional gender roles such as the gendered division of domestic labor, whereas women are drawn to more gender egalitarian attitudes in the new culture (Yoon et al., 2019). This divergence may lead to family conflict (Khawaja & Milner, 2012). Perhaps partly because of their role as cultural guardians, as women try to bridge their cultures of origin and their new cultures, they may feel guilt and shame about abandoning older cultural norms (Rashidian, Hussain, & Minichiello, 2013).

Despite expectations that they should be conservers of cultural traditions, women are not cultural prisoners. Rather, they have tended to seize opportunities to challenge norms that limit their choices. Less likely than men to endorse patriarchal beliefs (Yoon et al., 2015), women, as noted, have been a driving force behind cultural change that involves gendered roles and expectations. From the early British suffragists whose hunger strikes dramatized their determination to win voting rights, to the Afghan women who defied the Taliban's prohibition on girls' education by setting up secret schools, women have fought against their relegation to second-class status. From the Saudi women who challenged the driving ban, to the thousands of women who have participated in Women's Marches around the world, to the trio of female leaders in Belarus currently inspiring resistance to a dictatorial regime, many women have challenged restrictions based on gender. Refusing to conform to cultural dictates that limit their roles, they have instead sought to redefine expectations. Although cultural change with respect to gender norms and expectations has often been slow, there is clear evidence that it continues to take place in much of the world and that women are driving much of the change.

# References

Abalkhail, J. M. (2019). Women's career development in an Arab Middle Eastern context. *Human Resource Development International*, 22(2), 177–199. https://doi-org.lib-proxy.radford.edu/10.1080/13678868.2018.1499377

Abalkhail, J. M., & Allan, B. (2015). Women's career advancement: Mentoring and networking in Saudi Arabia and the UK. *Human Resource Development International*, *18*(2), 153–168. https://doi.org/10.1080/13678868.2015.1026548

Abrahams, N., Devries, K., Watts, C., Pallitto, C., Petzold, M., Shamu, S., & García-Moreno, C. (2014). Worldwide prevalence of non-partner sexual violence: A systematic review. *The Lancet*, *383*(9929), 1648–1654. https://doi.org/10.1016/S0140-6736(13)62243-6

Alhabib, S., Nur, U., & Jones, R. (2010). Domestic violence against women: Systematic review of prevalence studies. *Journal of Family Violence*, *25*(4), 369–382. https://doi.org/10.1007/s10896-009-9298-4

Allen, P. G. (1986). *The sacred hoop: Recovering the feminine in American Indian traditions*. Beacon Press.

Al-Modallal, H., Sowan, A. K., Hamaideh, S., Peden, A. R., Al-Omari, H., & Al-Rawashdeh, A. B. (2012). Psychological outcomes of intimate partner violence experienced by Jordanian working women. *Health Care for Women International*, *33*(3), 217–227. https://doi.org/10.1080/07399332.2011.610532

Alqout, O., & Reynolds, F. (2014). Experiences of obesity among Saudi Arabian women contemplating bariatric surgery: An interpretative phenomenological analysis. *Journal of Health Psychology*, *19*(5), 664–677. https://doi.org/10.1177/1359105313476977

Altschuler, J. (2017). Midlife and older women's experiences and advice about sex with men, risk behaviors, and HIV prevention education. *Journal of Women & Aging*, *29*(1), 63–74. https://doi.org/10.1080/08952841.2015.1063955

Amaral, A. C. S., & Ferreira, M. E. C. (2017). Body dissatisfaction and associated factors among Brazilian adolescents: A longitudinal study. *Body Image*, *22*, 32–38. https://doi.org/10.1016/j.bodyim.2017.04.006

Anderson-Fye, E. P. (2004). A 'Coca-Cola' shape: Cultural change, body image, and eating disorders in San Andrés, Belize. *Culture, Medicine and Psychiatry*, *28*, 561–595. http://doi.org/10.1007/s11013-004-1068-4.

Anuradha, C. S. (2008). Women political leadership and perception: A case study of South Asia. *International Journal of South Asian Studies*, *1*, 253–260. www.pondiuni.edu.in/sites/default/files/ijsas15062011_1.pdf

Aono, A., & Kashiwagi, K. (2011). III. Myth or fact: Conceptions and realities of Japanese women/mothers. *Feminism & Psychology, 21*(4), 516–521. https://doi.org/10.1177/0959353511422927

Apfelbaum, E. (1993). Norwegian and French women in high leadership positions: The importance of cultural context upon gendered relations. *Psychology of Women Quarterly,* 17, 409–429. http://dx.doi.org.lib-proxy .radford.edu/10.1111/j.1471-6402.1993.tb00653.x

Aranda, B., & Glick, P. (2014). Signaling devotion to work over family undermines the motherhood penalty. *Group Processes & Intergroup Relations, 17* (1), 91–99. https://doi.org/10.1177/1368430213485996

Arita, K. (2006). Lesbian mothers in Japan: An insider's report. *Journal of Lesbian Studies,* 10(3–4), 105–111. https://doi-org.lib-proxy.radford.edu/ 10.1300/J155v10n03_07

Arraf, J. (2020, August 2). Six years after the ISIS Yazidi genocide, one woman reflects. National Public Radio, Weekend Edition Sunday. www.npr.org/2020/ 08/02/898274873/six-years-after-the-isis-yazidi-genocide-one-woman-reflects

Astor, M. (2018, august 24). For female candidates, harassment and threats come every day. *The New York Times.* www.nytimes.com/2018/08/24/us/ politics/women-harassment-elections.html

Atske, S., Geiger, A. W., & Scheller, A. (2019, March 19). The share of women in legislatures around the world is growing, but they are still underrepresented. Fact-tank, Pew Research Center. www.pewresearch .org/fact-tank/

Backe, E. L., Lilleston, P., & McCleary-Sills, J. (2018). Networked individuals, gendered violence: A literature review of cyberviolence. *Violence and Gender, 5*(3), 135–146. https://doi.org/10.1089/vio.2017.0056

Bae, M. (2011). Interrogating girl power: Girlhood, popular media, and post-feminism. *Visual Arts Research, 37*(2), 28–40. http://dx.doi.org/ 10.5406/visualartsrese.37.2.0028

Baker, J. H. (2005). *Sisters: The lives of America's suffragists.* Farrar, Straus & Giroux.

Bankart, B. (1989). Japanese perceptions of motherhood. *Psychology of Women Quarterly, 13*(1), 59–76. https://doi.org/10.1111/j.1471–6402.1989.tb00985.x

Barbosa, G. N., Walker, B. B., Schuurman, N., Cavalcanti, S. D. L. B., Ferreira, E. F. e, & Ferreira, R. C. (2019). Epidemiological and spatial characteristics of interpersonal physical violence in a Brazilian city: A comparative study of violent injury hotspots in familial versus non-familial settings, 2012–2014. *PLoS ONE, 14*(1), Article e0208304. https://doi.org/10.1371/jour nal.pone.0208304

Barnawi, F. H. (2017). Prevalence and risk factors of domestic violence against women attending a primary care center in Riyadh, Saudi Arabia. *Journal of Interpersonal Violence, 32*(8), 1171–1186. https://doi.org/10.1177/0886260515587669

Batool, S. S., & de Visser, R. O. (2016). Experiences of infertility in British and Pakistani women: A cross-cultural qualitative analysis. *Health Care for Women International, 37*(2), 180–196. http://dx.doi.org/10.1080/07399332.2014.980890BBC News (September 28).

Beale, K., Malson, H., & Tischner, I. (2016). Deconstructing "real" women: Young women's readings of advertising images of "plus-size" models in the UK. *Feminism & Psychology, 26*(3), 378–386. https://doi.org/10.1177/0959353516639616

Beaman, L., Duflo, E., Rohini, P., & Topalova, P. (2012). Female leadership raises aspirations and educational attainment for girls: A policy experiment in India. *Science, 335*(6068), 582–586. http://doi.org/10.1126/science.1212382

Becker, A. E., Burwell, R. A., Herzog, D. B., Hamburg, P., & Gilman, S. E. (2002). Eating behaviours and attitudes following pro-longed exposure to television among ethnic Fijian adolescent girls. *The British Journal of Psychiatry, 180*(6), 509–514. https://doi.org/10.1192/bjp.180.6.509

Benard, S., & Correll, S. J. (2010). Normative discrimination and the motherhood penalty. *Gender & Society, 24*(5), 616–646. https://doi.org/10.1177/0891243210383142

Berhane, H. Y., Ekström, E.-C., Jirström, M., Berhane, Y., Turner, C., Alsanius, B. W., & Trenholm, J. (2018). Mixed blessings: A qualitative exploration of mothers' experience of child care and feeding in the rapidly urbanizing city of Addis Ababa, Ethiopia. *PLoS ONE, 13*(11), Article e0207685. https://doi.org/10.1371/journal.pone.0207685

Bermúdez, M. P., Matud, M. P., & Buela-Casal, G. (2009). Salud mental de las mujeres maltratadas por su pareja en El Salvador [Mental health of women battered by their partners in El Salvador]. *Revista Mexicana de Psicología, 26* (1), 51–59.

Bettinsoli, M. L., Suppes, A., & Napier, J. L. (2019, December 23). Predictors of attitudes toward gay men and lesbian women in 23 countries. *Social Psychological and Personality Science.* https://doi.org/10.1177/1948550619887785

Bhalerao, Y. P. (2019, August 4). Fragility and femininity: Reasons used to restrain women. shethepeople TV. www.shethepeople.tv/blog/fragility-femininity-women-working-night-shifts/

Bimha, P. Z. J., & Chadwick, R. (2016). Making the childfree choice: Perspectives of women living in South Africa. *Journal of Psychology in Africa, 26*(5), 449–456.

Black, M. C., Basile, K. C., Breiding, M. J., Smith, S.G., Walters, M. L., Merrick, M. T., Chen, J., & Stevens, M. R. (2011). *The National Intimate Partner and Sexual Violence Survey (NISVS): 2010 Summary Report.* National Center for Injury Prevention and Control, Centers for Disease Control and Prevention.

Blood, S. (2005). *Body work: The social construction of women's body image.* Routledge.

Bradshaw, Z., & slade, P. (2007). The relationships between induced abortion, attitudes towards sexuality and sexual problems. *Sexual and Relationship Therapy, 20*(4), 391–406.

Brescoll, V. L., Okimoto, T. G., & Vial, A. C. (2018). You've come a long way . . . maybe: How moral emotions trigger backlash against women leaders. *Journal of Social Issues, 74*(1), 144–164. https://doi.org/10.1111/josi.12261

Brown, A. W., & Gourdine, R. (2001). Black adolescent females: An examination of the impact of violence on their lives and perceptions of environmental supports. *Journal of Human Behavior in the Social Environment, 4*(4), 275–298. https://doi.org/10.1300/J137v04n04_04

Brown, L. M., & Gilligan, C. (1992). *Meeting at the crossroads: Women's psychology and girls' development.* Ballantine Books.

Budig, M. J., Misra, J., & Boeckmann, I. (2016). Work–family policy trade-offs for mothers? Unpacking the cross-national variation in motherhood earnings penalties. *Work and Occupations, 43*(2), 119–177. https://doi.org/10.1177/0730888415615385

Bünning, M. (2016). Die Vereinbarkeitsfrage für Männer: Welche Auswirkungen haben Elternzeiten und Teilzeitarbeit auf die Stundenlöhne von Vätern? [Work-family reconciliation for men: Do parental leave and part-time work affect fathers' hourly wages?]. *Kölner Zeitschrift für Soziologie und Sozialpsychologie, 68*(4), 597–618. https://doi.org/10.1007/s11577-016–0387-0

Burcar, L. (2018). High heels as a disciplinary practice of femininity in Sandra Cisneros's *The House on Mango Street. Journal of Gender Studies.* Advance online publication. https://doi.org/10.1080/09589236.2018.1472556

Burk, B. N., Pechenik Mausolf, A., & Oakleaf, L. (2020). Pandemic motherhood and the academy: A critical examination of the leisure-work dichotomy. *Leisure Sciences.* Advance online publication. https://doi.org/10.1080/01490400.2020.1774006

Burkett, E. (2015, June 6). What makes a woman? *The New York Times*. www
.nytimes.com/2015/06/07/opinion/sunday/what-makes-a-woman.html

Caffaro, F., Ferraris, F., & Schmidt, S. (2014). Gender differences in the
perception of honour killing in individualist versus collectivistic cultures:
Comparison between Italy and Turkey. *Sex Roles: A Journal of Research, 71*
(9–10), 296–318. https://doi.org/10.1007/s11199-014–0413-5

Cairns, K., Johnston, J., & MacKendrick, N. (2013). Feeding the "organic
child": Mothering through ethical consumption. *Journal of Consumer
Culture, 13*(2), 97–118. https://doi.org/10.1177/1469540513480162

Carli, L. L. (2017). Social influence and gender. In S. G. Harkins, K. D. Williams,
& J. M. Burger (Eds.), *Oxford library of psychology: The Oxford handbook of
social influence* (p. 33–51). Oxford University Press.

Carr, C. L. (2007). Where have all the tomboys gone? Women's accounts of
gender in adolescence. *Sex Roles: A Journal of Research, 56*(7–8), 439–448.
https://doi.org/10.1007/s11199-007–9183-7

Carter, C. (2016). Still sucked into the body image thing: The impact of anti-
aging and health discourses on women's gendered identities. *Journal of
Gender Studies, 25*, 200–214. http://doi.org/10.1080/09589236.2014.927354

Cases, J. G., Usaola, C. P., Aguado, F. G., Gironés, M. L., Trincado, M. R., &
Liria, A. F. (2014). Prevalence and characteristics of intimate partner violence against women with severe mental illness: A prevalence study in Spain.
*Community Mental Health Journal, 50*(7), 841–847. https://doi.org/10.1007/
s10597-014–9703-1

Cater, F. (2020, May 2). Federal judge dismisses U.S. women's soccer team's
equal pay claim. *NPR radio*. www.npr.org/2020/05/02/849492863/federal-
judge-dismisses-u-s-womens-soccer-team-s-equal-pay-claim

Center for Reproductive Rights (2020). *The World's Abortion Laws*. www
.worldabortionlaws.com/

Chalmers, B. (2012). Childbirth across cultures: Research and practice. *Birth:
Issues in Perinatal Care, 39*(4), 276–280. https://doi.org/10.1111/birt.12000

Chang, A. (2018, August 10). Japanese medical school admits to rigging
entrance exams to hurt women candidates. *NPR radio*. www.npr.org/2018/
08/10/637614700/japanese-medical-school-admits-to-rigging-entrance-
exams-to-hurt-women-candidate

Chesler, P. (2010). Worldwide trends in honor killings. *Middle East Quarterly,
17*(2), 3–11. www.meforum.org/2646/worldwide-trends-in-honor-killings

Chi, B. K., Rasch, V., Hạnh, N. T. T., & Gammeltoft, T. (2011). Pregnancy
decision-making among HIV positive women in Northern Vietnam:
Reconsidering reproductive choice. *Anthropology & Medicine, 18*(3),
315–326. https://doi.org/10.1080/13648470.2011.615909

Chiazor, I., Ozoya, M., Udume, M., & Egharevba, M. (2016). Taming the rape scourge in Nigeria: Issues and actions. *Gender and Behaviour*, 7764–7785.

Chzhen, Y., Gromada, A., & Rees, G. (2019). *Are the world's richest countries family friendly?: Policy in the OECD and EU*. UNICEF Office of Research.

Christnacht, C., & Sullivan, B. (2020, May 8). The choices working mothers make. US Census Bureau. www.census.gov/library/stories/2020/05/the-choices-working-mothers-make.html

Ciciolla, L., & Luthar, S. S. (2019). Invisible household labor and ramifications for adjustment: Mothers as captains of households. *Sex Roles: A Journal of Research, 81*(7–8), 467–486. https://doi.org/10.1007/s11199-018-1001-x

Cihangir, S. (2013). Gender specific honor codes and cultural change. *Group Processes & Intergroup Relations, 16*(3), 319–333. https://doi.org/10.1177/1368430212463453

Clark, C. J., Ferguson, G., Shrestha, B., Shrestha, P. N., Oakes, J. M., Gupta, J., McGhee, S., Cheong, Y. F., & Yount, K. M. (2018). Social norms and women's risk of intimate partner violence in Nepal. *Social Science & Medicine, 202*, 162–169. https://doi.org/10.1016/j.socscimed.2018.02.017

Clark, C. L., Glavin, K., Missal, B. E., & Sæteren, B. (2018). Is there a common experience? Somali new mothers' childbirth experiences in Norway and the United States. *Public Health Nursing, 35*(3), 184–191. https://doi.org/10.1111/phn.12399

Clayton, J. (2018, October 17). Sabarimala: Mobs attack women near India Hindu temple. BBC.com. www.bbc.com/news/world-asia-india-45885996

CNN Wire (2020, August 5). Turkish women rally against domestic violence as ruling party contemplates leaving key rights treaty. https://kfor.com/news/international/turkish-women-rally-against-domestic-violence-as-ruling-party-contemplates-leaving-key-rights-treaty/

Collins, C. (2020). Is maternal guilt a cross-national experience? *Qualitative Sociology*. Early access, April 2020. https://doi.org/10.1007/s11133-020-09451-2

Collins, C., Landivar, L. C., Ruppanner, L., & Scarborough, W. J. (2020). COVID-19 and the gender gap in work hours. *Gender, Work and Organization*. Advance online publication. https://doi.org/10.1111/gwao.12506

Coltrane, S., Miller, E. C., DeHaan, T., & Stewart, L. (2013). Fathers and the flexibility stigma. *Journal of Social Issues, 69*(2), 279–302. https://doi.org/10.1111/josi.12015

Cooke, L. P., & Fuller, S. (2018). Class differences in establishment pathways to fatherhood wage premiums. *Journal of Marriage and Family, 80*(3), 737–751. https://doi.org/10.1111/jomf.12475

Correll, S. J., Benard, S., & Paik, I. (2007). Getting a job: Is there a motherhood penalty? *American Journal of Sociology, 112*(5), 1297–1338. https://doi.org/10.1086/511799

Council on Foreign Relations (2020, May 22). *Women's Power Index.* www.cfr.org/article/womens-power-index

Crenshaw, K. (1991). Mapping the margins: Intersectionality, identity politics, and violence against women of color. *Stanford Law Review, 43,* 1241–1299. http://dx.doi.org/10.2307/1229039

Cuddy, A. J. C., Fiske, S. T., & Glick, P. (2004). When professionals become mothers, warmth doesn't cut the ice. *Journal of Social Issues, 60*(4), 701–718. https://doi.org/10.1111/j.0022–4537.2004.00381.x

Cunningham, J., & Macan, T. (2007). Effects of applicant pregnancy on hiring decisions and interview ratings. *Sex Roles: A Journal of Research, 57*(7–8), 497–508. https://doi.org/10.1007/s11199-007–9279-0

Currie, D. H. (1997). Decoding femininity: Advertisements and their teenage readers. *Gender & Society, 11,* 453–477.

Dashu, M. (1990). Women's Power. (DVD). Transcript accessed January 27, 2009. www.suppressedhistories.net/womenspowerscript3.html

del Mar Alonso-Almeida, M. (2014). Women (and mothers) in the workforce: Worldwide factors. *Women's Studies International Forum, 44,* 164–171. https://doi.org/10.1016/j.wsif.2014.01.010

de Pillis, E., Kernochan, R., Meilich, O., Prosser, E., & Whiting, V. (2008). Are managerial gender stereotypes universal? The case of Hawai'i. *Cross Cultural Management, 15*(1), 94–102. https://doi.org/10.1108/13527600810848854

DeRose, L. F., Goldscheider, F., Brito, J. R., Salazar-Arango, A., Corcuera, P., Corcuera, P. J., & Gas-Aixendri, M. (2019). Are children barriers to the gender revolution? International comparisons. *European journal of population, 35*(5), 987–1021. https://doi.org/10.1007/s10680-018–09515-8

Devries, K. M., Mak, J. Y. T., García-Moreno, C., Petzold, M., Child, J. C., Falder, G., Lim, S., Bacchus, L. J., Engell, R. E., Rosenfeld, L., Pallitto, C., Vos, T., Abrahams, N., & Watts, C. H. (2013). The global prevalence of intimate partner violence against women. *Science, 340*(6140), 1527–1528. https://doi.org/10.1126/science.1240937

Devries, K., Watts, C., Yoshihama, M., Kiss, L., Schraiber, L. B., Deyessa, N., Heise, L., Durand, J., Mbwambo, J., Jansen, H., Berhane, Y., Ellsberg, M., Garcia-Moreno, C., &WHO Multi-Country Study Team. (2011). Violence against women is strongly associated with suicide attempts: Evidence from the WHO multi-country study on women's health and domestic violence against women. *Social Science & Medicine, 73*(1), 79–86. https://doi.org/10.1016/j.socscimed.2011.05.006

Dharma, C., Lefebvre, D. L., Lu, Z., Lou, W. Y. W., Becker, A. B., Mandhane, P. J., Turvey, S. E., Moraes, T. J., Azad, M. B., Chen, E., Elliott, S. J., Kozyrskyj, A. L., Sears, M. R., & Subbarao, P. (2019). Risk for maternal depressive symptoms and perceived stress by ethnicities in Canada: From pregnancy through the preschool years. *The Canadian Journal of Psychiatry / La Revue canadienne de psychiatrie, 64*(3), 190–198. https://doi.org/10.1177/0706743718792190

Docan-Morgan, S. (2016). Cultural differences and perceived belonging during Korean adoptees' reunions with birth families. *Adoption Quarterly, 19*(2), 99–118. https://doi.org/10.1080/10926755.2015.1088109

Dodson, L. (2013). Stereotyping low-wage mothers who have work and family conflicts. *Journal of Social Issues, 69*(2), 257–278. https://doi.org/10.1111/josi.12014

Dunkel, T. M., Davidson, D., & Qurashi, S. (2010). Body satisfaction and pressure to be thin in younger and older Muslim and non-Muslim women: The role of Western and non-Western dress preferences. *Body Image, 7*(1), 56–65. https://doi.org/10.1016/j.bodyim.2009.10.003

Eagly, A. H., Makhijani, M. G., & Klonsky, B. G. (1992). Gender and the evaluation of leaders: A meta-analysis. *Psychological Bulletin, 111*(1), 3–22. https://doi.org/10.1037/0033-2909.111.1.3

Eaton, A. E., Jacobs, H., & Ruvalcaba, Y. (2017). 2017 *Nationwide online study of nonconsensual porn victimization and perpetration: A summary report.* Cyber Civil Rights Initiative, Florida International University. www.cybercivilrights.org/wp-content/uploads/2017/06/CCRI-2017-Research-Report.pdf

Eibach, J. (2016). Violence and masculinity. In P. Knepper & A. Johansen (Eds.), *The Oxford handbook of the history of crime* (pp. 229–249). Oxford University Press.

Elliott, C., & Stead, V. (2008). Learning from leading women's experience: Towards a sociological understanding. *Leadership, 4*(2), 159–180. https://doi.org/10.1177/1742715008089636

Elliott, S., & Bowen, S. (2018). Defending motherhood: Morality, responsibility, and double binds in feeding children. *Journal of Marriage and Family, 80*(2), 499–520. https://doi.org/10.1111/jomf.12465

Ellsberg, M., Jansen, H. A. F. M., Heise, L., Watts, C. H., García-Moreno, C., & WHO Multi-country Study on Women's Health and Domestic Violence against Women Study Team. (2008). Intimate partner violence and women's physical and mental health in the WHO multi-country study on women's health and domestic violence: An observational study. *The Lancet, 371*(9619), 1165–1172. https://doi.org/10.1016/S0140-6736(08)60522-X

Enander, V. (2010). "A fool to keep staying": Battered women labeling themselves stupid as an expression of gendered shame. *Violence Against Women, 16*(1), 5–31. https://doi.org/10.1177/1077801209353577

Endendijk, J. J., van Baar, A. L., & Deković, M. (2020). He is a stud, she is a slut! A meta-analysis on the continued existence of sexual double standards. *Personality and Social Psychology Review, 24*(2), 163–190. https://doi.org/10.1177/1088868319891310

England, P., Bearak, J., Budig, M. J., & Hodges, M. J. (2016). Do highly paid, highly skilled women experience the largest motherhood penalty?*American Sociological Review, 81*(6), 1161–1189. https://doi.org/10.1177/0003122416673598

Ennis, L. R. (Ed.) (2014). *Intensive mothering: The cultural contradictions of modern motherhood.* Demeter Press. http://doi.org/10.2307/j.ctt1rrd8rb

Felmlee, D., Inara Rodis, P., & Zhang, A. (2019). Sexist slurs: Reinforcing feminine stereotypes online. *Sex Roles: A Journal of Research.* Advance online publication. https://doi.org/10.1007/s11199-019-01095-z

Felski, R. (2006). "Because it is beautiful": New feminist perspectives on beauty. *Feminist Theory, 7*(2), 273–282. http://dx.doi.org/10.1177/1464700106064424

Ferrer-Pérez, V. A., & Bosch-Fiol, E. (2014). Gender violence as a social problem in Spain: Attitudes and acceptability. *Sex Roles: A Journal of Research, 70*(11–12), 506–521. https://doi.org/10.1007/s11199-013-0322-z

Ferris, E. G. (2007). Abuse of power: Sexual exploitation of refugee women and girls. *Signs, 32*(3), 584–591. https://doi.org/10.1086/510338

Fiaveh, D. Y., Izugbara, C. O., Okyerefo, M. P. K., Reysoo, F., & Fayorsey, C. K. (2015). Constructions of masculinity and femininity and sexual risk negotiation practices among women in urban Ghana. *Culture, Health & Sexuality, 17*(5), 650–662. https://doi.org/10.1080/13691058.2014.989264

Fielder, R. L., & Carey, M. P. (2010). Prevalence and characteristics of sexual hookups among first-semester female college students. *Journal of Sex & Marital Therapy, 36*, 346–359.doi:10.1080/0092623X.2010.488118

Fiske, S. T. (2017). Prejudices in cultural contexts: Shared stereotypes (gender, age) versus variable stereotypes (race, ethnicity, religion). *Perspectives on Psychological Science, 12*(5), 791–799. https://doi.org/10.1177/1745691617708204

Fleek, B. J. (2000). Native ways of knowing: experiences, influences and transitions of Tlingit women becoming leaders. *Masters Abstracts International, 38* (06), 1419.

Fontanesi, L., Marchetti, D., Mazza, C., Di Giandomenico, S., Roma, P., & Verrocchio, M. C. (2020). The effect of the COVID-19 lockdown on parents:

A call to adopt urgent measures. *Psychological Trauma: Theory, Research, Practice, and Policy*, *12*(S1), S79–S81. https://doi.org/10.1037/tra0000672

Forbes, G. B., Jung, J., Vaamonde, J. D., Omar, A., Paris, L., & Formiga, N. S. (2012). Body dissatisfaction and disordered eating in three cultures: Argentina, Brazil, and the U.S. *Sex Roles: A Journal of Research*, *66*(9–10), 677–694. https://doi.org/10.1007/s11199-011-0105-3

Forssén, A. S. K., Carlstedt, G., & Mörtberg, C. M. (2005). Compulsive sensitivity–a consequence of caring: A qualitative investigation into women carer's difficulties in limiting their labours. *Health Care for Women International*, *26*(8), 652–671. https://doi.org/10.1080/073993305 00177097

Forster, M. E., Palmer, F., & Barnett, S. (2016). Karanga mai ra: Stories of Māori women as leaders. *Leadership*, *12*(3), 324–345. https://doi.org/ 10.1177/1742715015608681

Fredrickson, B. L., & Roberts, T. (1997). Objectification theory: Toward under-standing women's lived experiences and mental health risks. *Psychology of Women Quarterly*, *21*, 173–206. https://doi:10.1111/j.1471-6402.1997 .tb00108.x

French, J. R. P. Jr., & Raven, B. H. (1959). The bases of social power. In D. Cartwright (Ed.), *Studies in social power* (pp. 150–167). University of Michigan Press.

Friedman, A., Tzukerman, Y., Wienberg, H., & Todd, J. (1992). The shift in power with age: Changes in perception of the power of women and men over the life cycle. *Psychology of Women Quarterly*, *16*, 513–525. https://doi.org/ 10.1111/j.1471–6402.1992.tb00272.x

Fritz, C., & van Knippenberg, D. (2017). Gender and leadership aspiration: Interpersonal and collective elements of cooperative climate differentially influence women and men. *Journal of Applied Social Psychology*, *47*(11), 591–604. https://doi.org/10.1111/jasp.12462

Fuller, S., & Hirsh, C. E. (2019). "Family-friendly" jobs and motherhood pay penalties: The impact of flexible work arrangements across the educational spectrum. *Work and Occupations*, *46*(1), 3–44. https://doi.org/10.1177/ 0730888418771116

Gambrell, K. M. (2016). Lakota women leaders: Getting things done quietly. *Leadership*, *12*(3), 293–307. https://doi.org/10.1177/1742715015608234

Garlough, C. L. (2008). On the political uses of folklore: Performance and grassroots feminist activism in India. *Journal of American Folklore*, *121* (480), 167–191.

Garlough, C. L. (2013). *Desi divas: Political activism in South Asian American cultural performances*. University Press of Mississippi.

Garousi, S., Garrusi, B., Baneshi, M. R., & Sharifi, Z. (2016). Weight management behaviors in a sample of Iranian adolescent girls. *Eating and Weight Disorders, 21*(3), 435–444. https://doi.org/10.1007/s40519-015-0249-1

Gartrell, N., Banks, A., Reed, N., Hamilton, J., Rodas, C., & Deck, A. (2000). The National Lesbian Family Study: 3. Interviews with mothers of five-year-olds. *American Journal of Orthopsychiatry, 70*(4), 542–548. https://doi.org/10.1037/h0087823

Gettleman, J. (2018, June 19). Where a taboo is leading to the deaths of young girls. *The New York Times.* www.nytimes.com/2018/06/19/world/asia/nepal-women-menstruation-period.html

Girard, M., Rodgers, R. F., & Chabrol, H. (2018). Prospective predictors of body dissatisfaction, drive for thinness, and muscularity concerns among young women in France: A sociocultural model. *Body Image, 26,* 103–110. https://doi.org/10.1016/j.bodyim.2018.07.001

Glass, C., & Fodor, E. (2018). Managing motherhood: Job context and employer bias. *Work and Occupations, 45*(2), 202–234. https://doi.org/10.1177/0730888417733521

Glauber, R. (2012). Women's work and working conditions: Are mothers compensated for lost wages? *Work and Occupations, 39*(2), 115–138. https://doi.org/10.1177/0730888411422948

Glauber, R. (2019). The wage penalty for parental caregiving: Has it declined over time? *Journal of Marriage and Family.* Advance online publication. https://doi.org/10.1111/jomf.12555

Glick, P. (2006). Ambivalent sexism, power distance, and gender inequality across cultures. In S. Guimond (Ed.), *Social comparison and social psychology: Understanding cognition, intergroup relations, and culture* (p. 283–302). Cambridge University Press.

Glick, P., Lameiras, M., Fiske, S. T., Eckes, T., Masser, B., Volpato, C., Manganelli, A. M., Pek, J. C. X., Huang, L.-l., Sakalli-Uğurlu, N., Castro, Y. R., D'Avila Pereira, M. L., Willemsen, T. M., Brunner, A., Six-Materna, I., & Wells, R. (2004). Bad but bold: Ambivalent attitudes toward men predict gender inequality in 16 nations. *Journal of Personality and Social Psychology, 86*(5), 713–728. https://doi.org/10.1037/0022-3514.86.5.713

Glynn, S. J. (2019, May 10). Breadwinning mothers continue to be the U.S. norm. Center for American Progress. www.americanprogress.org/issues/women/reports/2019/05/10/469739/breadwinning-mothers-continue-u-s-norm/

Golchin, N. A.. Hamzehgardeshi. Z, Fakhri, M., & Hamzehgardeshi, L. (2012). The experience of puberty in Iranian adolescent girls: A qualitative content analysis. *BMC Public Health, 12,* 698.

Gonçalves, M., & Matos, M. (2016). Prevalence of violence against immigrant women: A systematic review of the literature. *Journal of Family Violence, 31* (6), 697–710. https://doi.org/10.1007/s10896-016-9820-4

Gordon, A., & Glass, D. C. (1970). Choice ambiguity, dissonance, and defensiveness. *Journal of Personality, 38,* 264–272. https://doi.org/10.1111/j.1467–6494.1970.tb00008.x

Gracia, E., Lila, M., & Santirso, F. A. (2020). Attitudes toward intimate partner violence against women in the European Union: A systematic review. *European Psychologist, 25*(2), 104–121. https://doi.org/10.1027/1016–9040/a000392

Grant, M. J. (2012). Girls' schooling and the perceived threat of adolescent sexual activity in rural Malawi. *Culture, Health & Sexuality, 14,* 73–86. http://doi.org/10.1080/13691058.2011.624641

Grimshaw, D., & Rubery, J. (2015). *The motherhood pay gap: A review of the issues, theory and international evidence.* Geneva: International Labour Office. www.ilo.org/wcmsp5/groups/public/—dgreports/—dcomm/—publ/documents/publication/wcms_348041.pdf

Grogan, S. (2008). *Body image: Understanding body dissatisfaction in men, women, and children* (2nd ed.). Psychology Press.

Grose, R. G., Chen, J. S., Roof, K. A., Rachel, S., & Yount, K. M. (2020). Sexual and reproductive health outcomes of violence against women and girls in lower-income countries: A review of reviews. *Journal of Sex Research.* Advance online publication. https://doi.org/10.1080/00224499.2019.1707466

Gul, P., & Schuster, I. (2020). Judgments of marital rape as a function of honor culture, masculine reputation threat, and observer gender: A cross-cultural comparison between Turkey, Germany, and the UK. *Aggressive Behavior.* Advance online publication. https://doi.org/10.1002/ab.21893

Güney-Frahm, I. (2020). Neoliberal motherhood during the pandemic: Some reflections. *Gender, Work and Organization.* Advance online publication. https://doi.org/10.1111/gwao.12485

Guo, C., Pang, L., Wen, X., & Zheng, X. (2019). Risky sexual behaviors and repeat induced abortion among unmarried young women in China: Results from a large, nationwide, population-based sample. *Journal of Women's Health, 28*(10), 1442–1449.

Guppy, N., Sakumoto, L., & Wilkes, R. (2019). Social change and the gendered division of labor in Canada. *Canadian Review of Sociology, 2*(2), 178–203. https://doi.org/10.1111/cars.12242

Hall, L. J., & Donaghue, N. (2013). 'Nice girls don't carry knives': Constructions of ambition in media coverage of Australia's first female prime minister. *British Journal of Social Psychology, 52*(4), 631–647. https://doi.org/10.1111/j.2044-8309.2012.02114.x

Hanschmidt, F., Linde, K., Hilbert, A., Riedel-Heller, S. G., & Kersting, A. (2016). Abortion stigma: A systematic review. *Perspectives on Sexual and Reproductive Health, 48*(4), 169–177. https://doi.org/10.1363/48e8516

Hargreaves, D. A., & Tiggemann, M. (2004). Idealized media images and adolescent body image: "Comparing" boys and girls. *Body Image, 1*(4), 351–361. https://doi.org/10.1016/j.bodyim.2004.10.002

Harrison, R., Leitch, C., & McAdam, M. (2015). Breaking glass: Toward a gendered analysis of entrepreneurial leadership. *Journal of Small Business Management, 53*(3), 693–713. https://doi.org/10.1111/jsbm.12180

Harvey, V., & Tremblay, D.-G. (2018). Paternity leave in Québec: Between social objectives and workplace challenges. *Community, Work & Family, 23*, 253–269. https://doi.org/10.1080/13668803.2018.1527756

Hayman, B., & Wilkes, L. (2017). De novo families: Lesbian motherhood. *Journal of Homosexuality, 64*(5), 577–591. https://doi.org/10.1080/00918369.2016.1194119

Hays, S. (1996). *The cultural contradictions of motherhood.* Yale University Press.

Healy-Clancy, M. (2017). The family politics of the federation of South African women: A history of public motherhood in women's antiracist activism. *Signs: Journal of Women in Culture & Society, 42*(4), 843–867.

Heilman, M. E., & Caleo, S. (2018). Combatting gender discrimination: A lack of fit framework. *Group Processes & Intergroup Relations, 21*(5), 725–744. http://doi.org/10.1177/1368430218761587

Hennekam, S. A. M., & Ladge, J. J. (2017). When lesbians become mothers: Identity validation and the role of diversity climate. *Journal of Vocational Behavior, 103*(Part A), 40–55. https://doi.org/10.1016/j.jvb.2017.08.006

Herbert, A. C., Ramirez, A. M., Lee, G., North, S. J., Askari, M. S., West, R. L., & Sommer, M. (2017). Puberty experiences of low-income girls in the United States: A systematic review of qualitative literature from 2000 to 2014. *Journal of Adolescent Health, 60*(4), 363–379. https://doi.org/10.1016/j.jadohealth.2016.10.008

Hicken, M. T., Lee, H., Mezuk, B., Kershaw, K. N., Rafferty, J., & Jackson, J. S. (2013). Racial and ethnic differences in the association between obesity and depression in women. *Journal of Women's Health, 22*, 445–452. http://doi.org/10.1089/jwh.2012.4111.

Hicklin, A. (2014, April 8). Beyoncé liberated: Behind the scenes of the world's most powerful brand. Out.com. www.out.com/entertainment/music/2014/04/08/beyonc%C3%A9-liberated

Hideg, I., Krstic, A., Trau, R. N. C., & Zarina, T. (2018). The unintended consequences of maternity leaves: How agency interventions mitigate the negative effects of longer legislated maternity leaves. *Journal of Applied Psychology, 103*(10), 1155–1164. https://doi.org/10.1037/apl0000327

Hodges, M. J., & Budig, M. J. (2010). Who gets the daddy bonus?: Organizational hegemonic masculinity and the impact of fatherhood on earnings. *Gender & Society,* 24, 717–745. doi:http://dx.doi.org/10.1177/0891243210386729

Holloway, S. D., Suzuki, S., Yamamoto, Y., & Mindnich, J. D. (2006). Relation of maternal role concepts to parenting, employment choices, and life satisfaction among Japanese women. *Sex Roles: A Journal of Research, 54*(3–4), 235–249. https://doi.org/10.1007/s11199-006-9341-3

Holstein, M. (2015). *Women in later life: Critical perspectives on gender and age.* Rowman & Littlefield.

Holt, M. (2013). Violence against women in the context of war: Experiences of Shi'i women and Palestinian refugee women in Lebanon. *Violence Against Women, 19*(3), 316–337. https://doi.org/10.1177/1077801213485550

Hook, J. L. (2006). Care in context: Men's unpaid work in 20 countries, 1965–2003. *American Sociological Review,* 71, 639–660. https://doi-org.lib-proxy.radford.edu/10.1177/000312240607100406

Howard, J. A., & Gibson, M. A. (2019). Is there a link between paternity concern and female genital cutting in West Africa? *Evolution and Human Behavior, 40,* 1–11. https://doi.org/10.1016/j.evolhumbehav.2018.06.011

Hubbard, B. (2017, September 26). Saudi Arabia agrees to let women drive. *The New York Times.* www.nytimes.com/2017/09/26/world/middleeast/saudi-arabia-women-drive.html

Huda (2019, June 25). Why and when do Muslim girls wear the hijab? *Learn Religions.* www.learnreligions.com/when-do-muslim-girls-start-wearing-the-hijab-2004249

Human Rights Watch. (1996). *Shattered lives: Sexual violence during the Rwandan genocide and its aftermath.* New York: Human Rights Watch, Women's Rights Project. www.hrw.org/reports/1996/Rwanda.htm

Hyde, J. S., Bigler, R. S., Joel, D., Tate, C. C., & van Anders, S. M. (2019). The future of sex and gender in psychology: Five challenges to the gender binary. *American Psychologist, 74*(2), 171–193. https://doi.org/10.1037/amp0000307

Hyde, J. S., & Jaffee, S. R. (2000). Becoming a heterosexual adult: The experiences of young women. *Journal of Social Issues, 56,* 283–296.

Hynes, M., & Cardozo, B. L. (2000). Sexual violence against refugee women. *Journal of Women's Health & Gender-Based Medicine, 9*(8), 819–823. https://doi.org/10.1089/152460900750020847

Interligi, C. J., & McHugh, M. C. (2018). Women's sexuality: Victims, objects, or agents? In C. B. Travis & J.B White (Eds.), *APA Handbook of the Psychology of Women, Vol. 1. History, theory and battlegounds*. Washington, DC: American Psychological Association. pp 297–317.

International Labour Organization (2020). Maternity protection. www.social-protection.org/gimi/gess/ShowTheme.action?id=4425

Inter-Parliamentary Union (2016). *Sexual harassment and violence against women parliamentarians*. www.ipu.org/resources/publications/re-ports/2016-10/sexism-harassment-and-violence-against-women-parliamentarians

Inter-Parliamentary Union (2020). *Women in parliament: 1995–2020: 25 years in review*. www.ipu.org/resources/publications/reports/2020-03/women-in-parliament-1995-2020-25-years-in-review

Ipsos.com (2018, June 27). *Global views on cyberbullying*. www.ipsos.com/en/global-views-cyberbullying

Ivert, A.-K., Merlo, J., & Gracia, E. (2018). Country of residence, gender equality and victim blaming attitudes about partner violence: A multilevel analysis in EU. *European Journal of Public Health, 28*(3), 559–564. https://doi.org/10.1093/eurpub/ckx138

Jackson, T., Jiang, C., & Chen, H. (2016). Associations between Chinese/Asian versus Western mass media influences and body image disturbances of young Chinese women. *Body Image, 17*, 175–183. https://doi.org/10.1016/j.bodyim.2016.03.007

James-Hawkins, L., Cheong, Y. F., Naved, R. T., & Yount, K. M. (2018). Gender norms, violence in childhood, and men's coercive control in marriage: A multilevel analysis of young men in Bangladesh. *Psychology of Violence, 8*(5), 580–595. https://doi.org/10.1037/vio0000152

James-Hawkins, L., Salazar, K., Hennink, M. M., Ha, V. S., & Yount, K. M. (2019). Norms of masculinity and the cultural narrative of intimate partner violence among men in Vietnam. *Journal of Interpersonal Violence, 34*(21–22), 4421–4442. https://doi.org/10.1177/0886260516674941

Jang, S. J., Zippay, A., & Park, R. (2016). Family leave for employed women: Interaction effects of gender discrimination and household responsibilities in South Korea. *International Social Work, 59*(1), 99–114. https://doi.org/10.1177/0020872814531306

Jeffreys, S. (2005). *Beauty and misogyny: Harmful cultural practices in the West*. Routledge.

Joel, D., Tarrasch, R., Berman, Z., Mukamel, M., & Ziv, E. (2014). Queering gender: Studying gender identity in 'normative' individuals. *Psychology & Sexuality, 5*(4), 291–321.

Johansen, K. B. H., Pedersen, B. M., & Tjørnhøj-Thomsen, T. (2019). Visual gossiping: Non-consensual 'nude' sharing among young people in Denmark. *Culture, Health & Sexuality, 21*(9), 1029–1044. https://doi.org/10.1080/13691058.2018.1534140

Johnson, M. P. (1995). Patriarchal terrorism and common couple violence: Two forms of violence against women. *Journal of Marriage and the Family, 57,* 283–294. https://doi.org/10.1080/19419899.2013.830640

Johnson, M. P. (2008). *A typology of domestic violence: Intimate terrorism, violent resistance, and situational couple violence.* Northeastern University Press.

Jones, K. P., Peddie, C. I., Gilrane, V. L., King, E. B., & Gray, A. L. (2016). Not so subtle: A meta-analytic investigation of the correlates of subtle and overt discrimination. *Journal of Management, 42*(6), 1588–1613. https://doi.org/10.1177/0149206313506466

Jou, J., Kozhimannil, K. B., Abraham, J. M., Blewett, L. A., & McGovern, P. M. (2018). Paid maternity leave in the United States: Associations with maternal and infant health. *Maternal and Child Health Journal, 22*(2), 216–225. https://doi.org/10.1007/s10995-017-2393-x

Jung, J., & Forbes, G. B. (2007). Body dissatisfaction and disordered eating among college women in China, South Korea, and the United States: Contrasting predictions from sociocultural and feminist theories. *Psychology of Women Quarterly, 31*(4), 381–393. https://doi.org/10.1111/j.1471-6402.2007.00387.x

Jung, J., Forbes, G. B., & Lee, Y.-J. (2009). Body dissatisfaction and disordered eating among early adolescents from Korea and the US. *Sex Roles: A Journal of Research, 61*(1–2), 42–54. https://doi.org/10.1007/s11199-009-9609-5

Kan, M-Y. , & Laurie, H. (2016, January). Gender, ethnicity and household labour in married and cohabiting couples in the UK. Working paper No. 2016–01, Institute for Social & Economic Research, University of Essex. www.iser .essex.ac.uk/research/publications/working-papers/iser/2016-01.pdf

Karaman, E. R. (2016). Remember, s/he was here once. *Journal of Middle East Women's Studies, 12,* 382–411. http://doi.org/10.1215/15525864-3637576

Kasai, M., & Rooney, S. C. (2012). *The choice before the choice: Partner selection is essential to reproductive justice.* In J. C. Chrisler (Ed.), *Women's psychology. Reproductive justice: A global concern* (p. 11–28). Praeger/ABC-CLIO.

Kaufman, E. K., & Grace, P. E. (2011). Women in grassroots leadership: Barriers and biases experienced in a membership organization dominated by men. *Journal of Leadership Studies, 4*(4), 6–16. https://doi.org/10.1002/jls.20188

Kebede, M. T., Middelthon, A.-L., & Hilden, P. K. (2018). Negotiating the social and medical dangers of abortion in Addis Ababa: An exploration of young, unmarried women's abortion-seeking journeys. *Health Care for Women International, 39*(2), 186–207. https://doi.org/10.1080/07399332.2017.1388381

Kehoe, A.B. (1995). Blackfoot persons. In L. F. Klein & L. A. Ackerman (Eds.), *Women and power in native North America* (pp. 113–125). University of Oklahoma Press.

Kelmendi, K. (2015). Domestic violence against women in Kosovo: A qualitative study of women's experiences. *Journal of Interpersonal Violence, 30*(4), 680–702. https://doi.org/10.1177/0886260514535255

Kennedy, M. (2019, June 3). "Genocide" has been committed against indigenous women and girls, Canadian panel says. NPR Radio. www.npr.org/2019/06/03/729258906/genocide-has-been-committed-against-indigenous-women-and-girls-canadian-panel-sa

Kerrick, M. R., & Henry, R. L. (2017). "Totally in love": Evidence of a master narrative for how new mothers should feel about their babies. *Sex Roles, 76* (1–2), 1–16. http://dx.doi.org/10.1007/s11199-016-0666-2

Kertechian, S. K., & Swami, V. (2016). The hijab as a protective factor for body image and disordered eating: A replication in French Muslim women. *Mental Health, Religion & Culture, 19*(10), 1056–1068. https://doi.org/10.1080/13674676.2017.1312322

Kettrey, H. H. (2016). What's gender got to do with it? Sexual double standards and power in heterosexual college hookups. *Journal of Sex Research, 53*, 754–765. http://dx.doi.org/10.1080/00224499.2016.1145181

Keuroghlian, A. S., Shtasel, D., & Bassuk, E. L. (2014). Out on the street: A public health and policy agenda for lesbian, gay, bisexual, and transgender youth who are homeless. *American Journal of Orthopsychiatry, 84*, 66–72. http://doi.org/10.1037/h0098852

Keygnaert, I., Vettenburg, N., & Temmerman, M. (2012). Hidden violence is silent rape: Sexual and gender-based violence in refugees, asylum seekers and undocumented migrants in Belgium and the Netherlands. *Culture, Health & Sexuality, 14*(5), 505–520. https://doi.org/10.1080/13691058.2012.671961

Khalid, R. (1997). Perceived threat of violence & coping strategies: A case of Pakistan women. *Journal of Behavioural Sciences, 8*(1–2), 43–54.

Khawaja, N. G., & Milner, K. (2012). Acculturation stress in South Sudanese refugees: Impact on marital relationships. *International Journal of Intercultural Relations, 36*(5), 624–636. https://doi.org/10.1016/j.ijintrel.2012.03.007

Killeen, L. A., López-Zafram, E., & Eagly, A. H. (2006). Envisioning oneself as a leader: Comparisons of women and men in Spain and the United States. *Psychology of Women Quarterly, 30*, 312–322. http://dx.doi.org.lib-proxy.radford.edu/10.1111/j.1471-6402.2006.00299.x

Killewald, A. (2013). A reconsideration of the fatherhood premium: Marriage, coresidence, biology, and fathers' wages. *American Sociological Review, 78* (1), 96–116. https://doi.org/10.1177/0003122412469204

Kleisner, K., Kočnar, T., Tureček, P., Stella, D., Akoko, R. M., Třebický, V., & Havlíček, J. (2017). African and European perception of African female attractiveness. *Evolution and Human Behavior, 38*(6), 744–755. https://doi .org/10.1016/j.evolhumbehav.2017.07.002

Kleven, H., Landais, C., & Egholt Søgaard, J. (2019). Children and gender inequality: Evidence from Denmark. *American Economic Journal: Applied Economics, 11*, 181–209.

Knauss, C., Paxton, S. J., & Alsaker, F. D. (2008). Body dissatisfaction in adolescent boys and girls: Objectified body consciousness, internalization of the media body ideal and perceived pressure from media. *Sex Roles: A Journal of Research, 59*(9–10), 633–643. https://doi.org/10.1007/ s11199-008-9474-7

Koenig, A. M., Eagly, A. H., Mitchell, A. A., & Ristikari, T. (2011). Are leader stereotypes masculine? A meta-analysis of three research paradigms. *Psychological Bulletin, 137*(4), 616–642. http://doi.org/10.1037/a0023557

Koss, M. P., White, J. W., & Lopez, E. C. (2017). Victim voice in reenvisioning responses to sexual and physical violence nationally and internationally. *American Psychologist, 72*(9), 1019–1030. https://doi.org/10.1037/amp0000233

Kovacs, R. J. (2018). The macro-level drivers of intimate partner violence: New evidence from a multilevel dataset. *Global Public Health: An International Journal for Research, Policy and Practice, 13*(7), 944–956. https://doi.org/ 10.1080/17441692.2017.1317010

Kralik, J. (2016, July). School bathroom access for transgender students. *LegisBrief, 24*(26). Washington, DC: National Conference of State Legislatures. www.ncsl.org/research/education/school-bathroom-access-for-transgender-students.aspx

Krane, V., Choi, P. Y. L., Baird, S. M., Aimar, C. M., & Kauer, K. J. (2004). Living the paradox: Female athletes negotiate femininity and muscularity. *Sex Roles: A Journal of Research, 50*(5–6), 315–329. https://doi.org/10.1023/ B:SERS.0000018888.48437.4f

Kurtzleben, D. (2020, July 28). What the "Wall of Moms" protests say about motherhood, race in America. *NPR radio.* www.npr.org/2020/07/28/ 896174019/what-the-wall-of-moms-protests-say-about-motherhood-race-in-america

Lamb, S., & Peterson, Z. D. (2012). Adolescent girls' sexual empowerment: Two feminists explore the concept. *Sex Roles: A Journal of Research, 66* (11–12), 703–712. https://doi.org/10.1007/s11199-011-9995-3

Lauri Korajlija, A., & Jokic-Begic, N. (2020). COVID-19: Concerns and behaviours in Croatia. *British Journal of Health Psychology*. Advance online publication. https://doi.org/10.1111/bjhp.12425

Lawson, K. M., & Lips, H. M. (2014). The role of self-perceived agency and job attainability in women's impressions of successful women in masculine occupations. *Journal of Applied Social Psychology, 44*(6), 433–441. https://doi.org/10.1111/jasp.12236

Le Renard, A. (2013). Young urban Saudi women's transgressions of official rules and the production of a new social group. *Journal of Middle East Women's Studies, 9*(3), 108–135. http://doi.org/10.2979/jmiddeastwomstud.9.3.108

Leahey, T. M., Crowther, J. H., & Mickelson, K. D. (2007). The frequency, nature, and effects of naturally occurring appearance-focused social comparisons. *Behavior Therapy, 38*, 132–143.

Lee, H.-R., Lee, H. E., Choi, J., Kim, J. H., & Han, H. L. (2014). Social media use, body image, and psychological well-being: A cross-cultural comparison of Korea and the United States. *Journal of Health Communication, 19*(12), 1343–1358. https://doi.org/10.1080/10810730.2014.904022

Lee, W. L. (2010). *Contemporary feminist theory and activism: Six global issues*. Peterborough, Ontario: Broadview Press.

Lemish, D., & Muhlbauer, V. (2012). "Can't have it all": Representations of older women in popular culture. *Women & Therapy, 35*(3–4), 165–180. https://doi.org/10.1080/02703149.2012.684541

Leskinen, E. A., Rabelo, V. C., & Cortina, L. M. (2015). Gender stereotyping and harassment: A "catch-22" for women in the workplace. *Psychology, Public Policy, and Law, 21*(2), 192–204. https://doi.org/10.1037/law0000040

Levanon, A., England, P., & Allison, P. (2009). Occupational feminization and pay: Assessing causal dynamics using 1950–2000 U.S. Census data. *Social Forces, 88*(2), 865–891. http://doi.org/10.1353/sof.0.0264

Li, M., Turki, N., Izaguirre, C. R., DeMahy, C., Thibodeaux, B. L., & Gage, T. (2020). Twitter as a tool for social movement: An analysis of feminist activism on social media communities. *Journal of Community Psychology*. Advance online publication. https://doi.org/10.1002/jcop.22324

Lin, K., Sun, I. Y., Wu, Y., & Liu, J. (2016). College students' attitudes toward intimate partner violence: A comparative study of China and the U.S. *Journal of Family Violence, 31*(2), 179–189. https://doi.org/10.1007/s10896-015-9759-x

Linde Leonard, M., & Stanley, T. D. (2020). The wages of mothers' labor: A meta-regression analysis. *Journal of Marriage and Family*. Advance online publication. https://doi.org/10.1111/jomf.12693

Lips, H. M. (2000). College students' visions of power and possibility as moderated by gender. *Psychology of Women Quarterly*, *24*(1), 39–43. https://doi.org/10.1111/j.1471–6402.2000.tb01020.x

Lips, H. M. (2001). Envisioning positions of leadership: The expectations of university students in Virginia and Puerto Rico. *Journal of Social Issues*, 57(4), 799–813. https://doi-org.lib-proxy.radford.edu/10.1111/0022-4537.00242

Lips, H. M. (2018). *Feminism, psychology, and the gender pay gap*. In C. B. Travis, J. W. White, A. Rutherford, W. S. Williams, S. L. Cook, & K. F. Wyche (Eds.), *APA handbooks in psychology®. APA handbook of the psychology of women: History, theory, and battlegrounds* (p. 417–433). Washington, DC: American Psychological Association. https://doi.org/10.1037/0000059–021

Livingston, G. (2013), December 20). The link between parental leave and the gender pay gap. *FactTank*, Pew Research Center. www.pewresearch.org/fact-tank/2013/12/20/the-link-between-parental-leave-and-the-gender-pay-gap/

Livingstone, S., Haddon, L., Görzig, A., & Ólafsson, K. (2011). *Risks and safety on the internet: The perspective of European children: Full findings and policy implications from the EU Kids Online survey of 9–16 year olds and their parents in 25 countries*. EU Kids Online, Deliverable D4. EU Kids Online Network, London, UK. http://eprints.lse.ac.uk/33731/

Lokot, T. (2018). #IAmNotAfraidToSayIt: Stories of sexual violence as everyday political speech on Facebook. *Information, Communication & Society*, *21*(6), 802–817. https://doi.org/10.1080/1369118X.2018.1430161

Luo, Y.-j., Jackson, T., Niu, G.-f., & Chen, H. (2020). Effects of gender and appearance comparisons on associations between media-based appearance pressure and disordered eating: Testing a moderated mediation model. *Sex Roles: A Journal of Research*, *82*(5/6), 293–305. Advance online publication. https://doi.org/10.1007/s11199-019–01058-4

Magnusson, C. (2019). Flexible time – but is the time owned? Family friendly and family unfriendly work arrangements, occupational gender composition and wages: A test of the mother-friendly job hypothesis in Sweden. *Community, Work & Family*. Advance online publication. https://doi.org/10.1080/13668803.2019.1697644

Mahdavi, P. (2009). "But what if someone sees me?" Women, risk, and the aftershocks of Iran's sexual revolution. *Journal of Middle East Women's Studies*, *5*(2), 1–22. http://doi.org/10.2979/MEW.2009.5.2.1

Malchik, A. (2020, February 14). The neglected consequences of foot-binding: Just how much is society willing to damage women in order to control them? *The Atlantic*. www.theatlantic.com/health/archive/2020/02/lasting-damage-foot-binding/606439/

Malson, H. (1998).*The thin woman: Feminism, post-structuralism and the social psychology of anorexia nervosa*. Routledge.

Mann, E. S., Cardona, V., & Gómez, C. A. (2015). Beyond the discourse of reproductive choice: Narratives of pregnancy resolution among Latina/o teenage parents. *Culture, Health & Sexuality, 17*(9), 1090–1104. https://doi .org/10.1080/13691058.2015.1038853

Marketplace.org (2008, March 12). Saudi boy meets girl – via Bluetooth. www .marketplace.org/2008/03/12/saudi-boy-meets-girl-bluetooth/

Marks, M. J., Young, T. M., & Zaikman, Y. (2019). The sexual double standard in the real world: Evaluations of sexually active friends and acquaintances. *Social Psychology, 50*(2), 67–79. https://doi.org/10.1027/1864–9335/ a000362

Martin, J. L., & Smith, J. (2020). Why we march! Feminist activism in critical times: Lessons from the Women's March on Washington. *Women's Studies International Forum, 81*, Article 102375. https://doi.org/10.1016/j .wsif.2020.102375

Martinez-Marcos, M., & De la Cuesta-Benjumea, C. (2014). How women care-givers deal with their own long-term illness: A qualitative study. *Journal of Advanced Nursing, 70*(8), 1825–1836. https://doi.org/10.1111/jan.12341

Mashal, M. (2020, July 20). For women in Afghan security forces, a daily battle. *New York Times.* www.nytimes.com/2020/07/20/world/asia/afghanistan-women-police.html?auth=login-email&login=email

Matud, M. P. (2005). The psychological impact of domestic violence on Spanish women. *Journal of Applied Social Psychology, 35*(11), 2310–2322. https:// doi.org/10.1111/j.1559–1816.2005.tb02104.x

McCloskey, J. (2007). *Living through the generations: Continuity and change in Navajo women's lives*. University of Arizona Press.

McDermott, R. C., Kilmartin, C., McKelvey, D. K., & Kridel, M. M. (2015). College male sexual assault of women and the psychology of men: Past, present, and future directions for research. *Psychology of Men & Masculinity, 16*(4), 355–366. https://doi.org/10.1037/a0039544

McGregor, J., & Davies, S. G. (2019). Achieving pay equity: Strategic mobil-ization for substantive equality in Aotearoa New Zealand. *Gender, Work and Organization, 26*(5), 619–632. https://doi.org/10.1111/gwao.12253

Mehta, N., Baum, S. E., Cartwright, A. F., Cockrill, K., & Upadhyay, U. D. (2019). The association between reproductive autonomy and abortion stigma among women who have had abortions in the United States. *Stigma and Health, 4*(4), 377–382. https://doi.org/10.1037/sah0000151

Mellor, D., Waterhouse, M., Mamat, N. H. b., Xu, X., Cochrane, J., McCabe, M., & Ricciardelli, L. (2013). Which body features are associated with female adolescents' body dissatisfaction? A cross-cultural study in Australia, China and Malaysia. *Body Image, 10*(1), 54–61. https://doi.org/10.1016/j.bodyim.2012.10.002

Mendes, K., Ringrose, J., & Keller, J. (2018). #MeToo and the promise and pitfalls of challenging rape culture through digital feminist activism. *European Journal of Women's Studies, 25*(2), 236–246. https://doi.org/10.1177/1350506818765318

Miller, B. D. (1997). *The endangered sex: Neglect of female children in rural North India* (2nd edition). New York: Oxford University Press.

Miyajima, T., & Yamaguchi, H. (2017). I want to but I won't: Pluralistic ignorance inhibits intentions to take paternity leave in Japan. *Frontiers in Psychology, 8*, Article 1508. https://doi.org/10.3389/fpsyg.2017.01508

Moreno-Colom, S. (2017). The gendered division of housework time: Analysis of time use by type and daily frequency of household tasks. *Time & Society, 26*, 3–27. https://doi:10.1177/0961463X15577269

Morgenroth, T., & Heilman, M. E. (2017). Should I stay or should I go? Implications of maternity leave choice for perceptions of working mothers. *Journal of Experimental Social Psychology, 72*, 53–56. https://doi.org/10.1016/j.jesp.2017.04.008

Mueller, J., & Sherr, L. (2009). Abandoned babies and absent policies. *Health Policy, 93*(2–3), 157–164. https://doi.org/10.1016/j.healthpol.2009.06.002

Munala, L., Welle, E., Hohenshell, E., & Okunna, N. (2018). "She is NOT a genuine client": Exploring health practitioner's mistrust of rape survivors in Nairobi, Kenya. *International Quarterly of Community Health Education, 38*(4), 217–224. https://doi.org/10.1177/0272684X18781790

Murnen, S. K., Wright, C., & Kaluzny, G. (2002). If "boys will be boys," then girls will be victims? A meta-analytic review of the research that relates masculine ideology to sexual aggression. *Sex Roles: A Journal of Research, 46*(11–12), 359–375. https://doi.org/10.1023/A:1020488928736

Musaiger, A. O., D'Souza, R., & Al-Roomi, K. (2013). Perception of ageing and ageism among women in Qatar. *Journal of Women & Aging, 25*, 273–280. https://doi.org/10.1080/08952841.2013.791602

Nappi, R. E., Abascal, P. L., Mansour, D., Rabe, T., Shojai, R., and Emergency Contraception Study Group. (2014). Use of and attitudes towards emergency contraception: A survey of women in five European countries. *The European Journal of Contraception and Reproductive Health Care, 19*(2), 93–101. https://doi.org/10.3109/13625187.2013.865164

Nasrullah, M., Haqqi, S., & Cummings, K. J. (2009). The epidemiological patterns of honour killing of women in Pakistan. *European Journal of Public Health, 19*(2), 193–197. https://doi.org/10.1093/eurpub/ckp021

National Coalition for Women & Girls in Education (2017). Title IX at 45: Advancing opportunity through equity in education. http://ncwge.org/ TitleIX45/Title%20IX%20at%2045-Advancing%20Opportunity% 20through%20Equity%20in%20Education.pdf

Naylor, H. (2016, March 12). Love, Saudi Arabian style. *Washington Post.* www.washingtonpost.com/world/middle_east/saudis-look-for-love-and-lust–and-find-it–on-social-media/2016/03/11/ad584410-67da-4501–9457-987c7cf6f534_story.html

Netchaeva, E., Kouchaki, M., & Sheppard, L. D. (2015). A man's (precarious) place: Men's experienced threat and self-assertive reactions to female superiors. *Personality and Social Psychology Bulletin, 41*(9), 1247–1259. https:// doi.org/10.1177/0146167215593491

Newman, S. (2017, November 27). The roots of infanticide. *Psyche.* https:// aeon.co/essays/the-roots-of-infanticide-run-deep-and-begin-with-poverty

Nikniaz, Z., Mahdavi, R., Amiri, S., Ostadrahimi, A., & Nikniaz, L. (2016). Factors associated with body image dissatisfaction and distortion among Iranian women. *Eating Behaviors, 22,* 5–9. https://doi.org/10.1016/ j.eatbeh.2016.03.018

Niu, G., Sun, L., Liu, Q., Chai, H., Sun, X., & Zhou, Z. (2020). Selfie-posting and young adult women's restrained eating: The role of commentary on appearance and self-objectification. *Sex Roles: A Journal of Research.* Advance online publication. https://doi.org/10.1007/s11199-019–01045-9

Niu, X., & Laidler, K. A. J. (2015). Understanding domestic violence against Muslim women in China. *Feminist Criminology, 10*(1), 92–112. https://doi .org/10.1177/1557085114536766

North, A. (2017, September 22). Can transgender students go to women's colleges? The answer is evolving. *Vox.* www.vox.com/identities/2017/9/21/ 16315072/spelman-college-transgender-students-womens-colleges

Nzegwu, N. (2004). The epistemological challenge of motherhood to patriliny. *JENdA: A Journal of Culture and African Women Studies,* 5. Retrieved January 19, 2009 from www.jendajournal.com/issue5/nzegwu.htm

Oberg, P., & Tornstam, L. (2003). Attitudes toward embodied old age among Swedes. *International Journal of Aging & Human Development, 56,* 133–153.

Obiyan, M., & Agunbiade, O. (2014). Paradox of parental involvement in sexual health and induced abortions among in-school female adolescents in southwest Nigeria. *Sexuality & Culture, 18*(4), 847–869.

O'Donnell, V., & Wallace, S. (2011). *Women in Canada: A gender-based statistical report: First Nations, Inuit and Métis Women.* Statistics Canada. www.statcan.gc.ca/pub/89–503-x/2010001/article/11442-eng.pdf

Okimoto, T. G., & Brescoll, V. L. (2010). The price of power: Power seeking and backlash against female politicians. *Personality and Social Psychology Bulletin, 36*(7), 923–936. https://doi.org/10.1177/0146167210371949 ˙

Onyejekwe, C. J. (2008). Nigeria: The dominance of rape. *Journal of International Women's Studies, 10*(1), 48–64.

Organization for Economic Co-operation and Development (2012, December 17). *Lack of support for motherhood hurting women's career prospects, despite gains in education and employment, says OECD.* News release. www.oecd.org/newsroom/lackofsupportformotherhoodhurtingwomen scareerprospectsdespitegainsineducationandemploymentsaysoecd.htm

Organization for Economic Co-operation and Development (2019). Incomes and poverty of older people. In *Pensions at a glance 2019. OECD and G20 indicators.* www.oecd.org/pensions/oecd-pensions-at-a-glance-19991363 .htm

Organization for Economic Co-operation and Development (2020). Stat. Employment: Time spent in paid and unpaid work, by sex. Accessed July 14, 2020. https://stats.oecd.org/index.aspx?queryid=54757#&te=1&nl=in-her%20words&emc=edit_gn_20200123?campaign_id=10&instance_id=15395& segment_id=20585&user_id=b656c071f8dcd1ae8c40e33510daeeef&re gi_id=85364281_gn_20200123

Pachankis, J. E., & Bränström, R. (2018). Hidden from happiness: Structural stigma, sexual orientation concealment, and life satisfaction across 28 countries. *Journal of Consulting and Clinical Psychology, 86*(5), 403–415. https://doi.org/10.1037/ccp0000299

Parks-Stamm, E. J., Heilman, M. E., & Hearns, K. A. (2008). Motivated to penalize: Women's strategic rejection of successful women. *Personality and Social Psychology Bulletin, 34*(2), 237–247. https://doi.org/10.1177/0146167207310027

Paustian-Underdahl, S. C., Eaton, A. A., Mandeville, A., & Little, L. M. (2019). Pushed out or opting out? Integrating perspectives on gender differences in withdrawal attitudes during pregnancy. *Journal of Applied Psychology, 104*(8), 985–1002. https://doi.org/10.1037/apl0000394

Petit, M.-P., Julien, D., & Chamberland, L. (2017). Negotiating parental designations among trans parents' families: An ecological model of parental identity. *Psychology of Sexual Orientation and Gender Diversity, 4*(3), 282–295. https://doi.org/10.1037/sgd0000231

Petit, M.-P., Julien, D., & Chamberland, L. (2018). Interlinkages between parental and trans trajectories: A life course perspective. *Psychology of Sexual Orientation and Gender Diversity, 5*(3), 371–386. https://doi.org/10.1037/sgd0000280

Phelan, J.E., & Rudman, L. A. (2010). Prejudice toward female leaders: Backlash effects and women's impression management dilemma. *Social and Personality Psychology Compass,* 4(10), 807–820. https://doi: 0.1111/j.1751-9004.2010.00306.x

Pipher, M. (1994). *Reviving Ophelia: Saving the selves of adolescent girls.* Riverhead Books.

Piran, N. (2016). Embodied possibilities and disruptions: The emergence of the experience of embodiment construct from qualitative studies with girls and women. *Body Image, 18,* 43–60. http://dx.doi.org/10.1016/j.bodyim.2016.04.007

Piran, N. (2017). *Journeys of embodiment at the intersection of body and culture: The developmental theory of embodiment.* Elsevier Academic Press.

Player, A., Randsley de Moura, G., Leite, A. C., Abrams, D., & Tresh, F. (2019). Overlooked leadership potential: The preference for leadership potential in job candidates who are men vs. women. *Frontiers in Psychology, 10,* Article 755. https://doi.org/10.3389/fpsyg.2019.00755

Poloskov, E., & Tracey, T. J. G. (2013). Internalization of U.S. female beauty standards as a mediator of the relationship between Mexican American women's acculturation and body dissatisfaction. *Body Image, 10*(4), 501–508. https://doi.org/10.1016/j.bodyim.2013.05.005

Poonam, S. (2019, January 3). Indian women just did a remarkable thing – they formed a wall of protest. *The Guardian.* www.theguardian.com/commentis free/2019/jan/03/gender-activism-india-womens-wall-sabarimala-temple-kerala

Popper-Giveon, A. (2009, May). Adapted traditions: The case of traditional Palestinian women healers in Israel. *Forum: Qualitative Social Research, 10*(2). www.qualitative-research.net/index.php/fqs/article/view/1205/2726

Power, T., Jackson, D., Weaver, R., & Carter, B. (2011). Social support for mothers in illness: A multifaceted phenomenon. *Contemporary Nurse, 40*(1), 27–40. https://doi.org/10.5172/conu.2011.40.1.27

Prime, J., Jonsen, K., Carter, N., & Maznevski, M. L. (2008). Managers' perceptions of women and men leaders: A cross cultural comparison. *International Journal of Cross Cultural Management, 8*(2), 171–210. https://doi.org/10.1177/1470595808091789

Rashidian, M., Hussain, R., & Minichiello, V. (2013). "My culture haunts me no matter where I go": Iranian-American women discussing sexual and acculturation experiences. *Culture, Health & Sexuality, 15*(7), 866–877. https://doi.org/10.1080/13691058.2013.789128

Rajagopalan, S., & Tabarrok, A. T. (2019). Premature imitation and India's flailing state. *The Independent Review: A Journal of Political Economy, 24*(2), 165–186.

Razali, S., Kirkman, M., Ahmad, S. H., & Fisher, J. (2014). Infanticide and illegal infant abandonment in Malaysia. *Child Abuse & Neglect, 38*(10), 1715–1724. https://doi.org/10.1016/j.chiabu.2014.06.008

Reisner, S. L., Poteat, T., Keatley, J., Cabral, M., Mothopeng, T., Dunham, E., Holland, C. E., Max, R., & Baral, S. D. (2016). Global health burden and needs of transgender populations: A review. *Lancet (London, England), 388* (10042), 412–436. https://doi.org/10.1016/S0140-6736(16)00684-X

Rice, C. (2014). *Becoming women: The embodied self in image culture.* University of Toronto Press.

Riley, S. C. E., & Scharff, C. (2013). Feminism versus femininity? Exploring feminist dilemmas through cooperative inquiry research. *Feminism & Psychology, 23*(2), 207–223. https://doi.org/10.1177/0959353512454615

Robertson, L. G., Anderson, T. L., Hall, M. E. L., & Kim, C. L. (2019). Mothers and mental labor: A phenomenological focus group study of family-related thinking work. *Psychology of Women Quarterly, 43*(2), 184–200. https://doi.org/10.1177/0361684319825581

Rogers Wood, N. A., & Petrie, T. A. (2010). Body dissatisfaction, ethnic identity, and disordered eating among African American women. *Journal of Counseling Psychology, 57*(2), 141–153. https://doi.org/10.1037/a0018922

Rongmuang, D., Corte, C., McCreary, L. L., Park, C. G., Miller, A., & Gallo, A. (2011). Salience of physical appearance characteristics among young women in Thailand. *Body Image, 8*(4), 396–403. https://doi.org/10.1016/j.bodyim.2011.05.004

Rowe, D. (2014). Sport, media and the gender-based insult. In C. Carter, L. Steiner, & L. McLaughlin (Eds.), *Routledge Companion to Media and Gender* (pp.395–405). Routledge.

Rudman, L. A., Moss-Racusin, C. A., Glick, P., & Phelan, J. E. (2012). Reactions to vanguards: Advances in backlash theory. In P. G. Devine & E. A. Plant (Eds.), *Advances in experimental social psychology* (Vol. 45, pp. 167–227). Cambridge, MA: Academic Press. http://dx.doi.org/10.1016/B978-0-12-394286-9.00004-4

Rudman, L. A., Moss-Racusin, C. A., Phelan, J. E., & Nauts, S. (2012). Status incongruity and backlash effects: Defending the gender hierarchy motivates prejudice against female leaders. *Journal of Experimental Social Psychology, 48*(1), 165–179. https://doi.org/10.1016/j.jesp.2011.10.008

Sanday, P. R. (1981). The socio-cultural context of rape: A cross-cultural study. *Journal of Social Issues, 37*, 5–27.

Sanday, P. R. (2003). Rape-free versus rape-prone: How culture makes a difference. In C. B. Travis (Ed.), *Evolution, gender, and rape* (pp. 337–361). MIT Press.

Sardinha, L., & Catalán, H. E. N. (2018). Attitudes towards domestic violence in 49 low- and middle-income countries: A gendered analysis of prevalence and country-level correlates. *PLOS One, 13*(10), e0206101. https://doi.org/10.1371/journal.pone.0206101

Scott, L. (2005). *Fresh lipstick: Redressing fashion and feminism.* Palgrave.

Sebastian, M. (2016, July 26). Who are the 'Mothers of the Movement' speaking at the Democratic National Convention? *Elle.* www.elle.com/culture/career-politics/news/a38111/who-are-mothers-of-the-movement-dnc/

Semley, L. (2012). Public motherhood in West Africa as theory and practice. *Gender & History, 24,* 600–616. https://doi.org/10.1111/j.1468-0424.2012.01698.x

Scheper-Hughes, N. (1985). Culture, scarcity, and maternal thinking: Maternal detachment and infant survival in a Brazilian shantytown. *Ethos, 13,* 291–317.

Scheper-Hughes, N. (1992). *Death without weeping: The violence of everyday life in Brazil.* University of California Press.

Shakib, S. (2003). Female basketball participation: Negotiating the conflation of peer status and gender status from childhood through puberty. *American Behavioral Scientist, 46,* 1405–1422.

Shahawy, S., & Diamond, M. B. (2018). Perspectives on induced abortion among Palestinian women: Religion, culture and access in the occupied Palestinian territories. *Culture, Health & Sexuality, 20*(3), 289–305. https://doi.org/10.1080/13691058.2017.1344301

Sheldon, S. (2018). Empowerment and Privacy? Home Use of Abortion Pills in the Republic of Ireland. *Signs: Journal of Women in Culture & Society, 43*(4), 823–849.

Sheppard, L. D. (2018). Gender differences in leadership aspirations and job and life attribute preferences among U.S. undergraduate students. *Sex Roles: A Journal of Research, 79*(9–10), 565–577. https://doi.org/10.1007/s11199-017-0890-4

Shostak, M. (1981). *Nisa: The life and words of a !Kung woman.* Vintage.

Shloim, N., Hugh-Jones, S., Rudolf, M. C. J., Feltbower, R. G., Lans, O., & Hetherington, M. M. (2015). "It's like giving him a piece of me": Exploring UK and Israeli women's accounts of motherhood and feeding. *Appetite, 95,* 58–66. https://doi.org/10.1016/j.appet.2015.06.004

Shroff, H., & Thompson, J. K. (2006). Peer Influences, body-image dissatisfaction, eating dysfunction and self-esteem in adolescent girls. *Journal of Health Psychology, 11*(4), 533–551. https://doi.org/10.1177/1359105306065015

Sidani, Y. M., Konrad, A., & Karam, C. M. (2015). From female leadership advantage to female leadership deficit: A developing country perspective.

*The Career Development International, 20*(3), 273–292. https://doi.org/10.1108/CDI-01-2014-0009

Sinclair, S., Carlsson, R., & Björklund, F. (2016). Getting along or ahead: Effects of gender identity threat on communal and agentic self-presentations. *Scandinavian Journal of Psychology, 57*(5), 427–432. https://doi.org/10.1111/sjop.12310

Sisson, G. (2015). "Choosing life": Birth mothers on abortion and reproductive choice. *Women's Health Issues, 25*(4), 349–354. https://doi.org/10.1016/j.whi.2015.05.007

Smith, D. G., Rosenstein, J. E., Nikolov, M. C., & Chaney, D. A. (2019). The power of language: Gender, status, and agency in performance evaluations. *Sex Roles: A Journal of Research, 80*(3–4), 159–171. https://doi.org/10.1007/s11199-018-0923-7

Smith, J. L., & Huntoon, M. (2013). Women's bragging rights: Overcoming modesty norms to facilitate women's self-promotion. *Psychology of Women Quarterly. 38*(4), 447–459. http://doi.org/10.1177/0361684313515

Smith, R. M., Parrott, D. J., Swartout, K. M., & Tharp, A. T. (2015). Deconstructing hegemonic masculinity: The roles of antifemininity, subordination to women, and sexual dominance in men's perpetration of sexual aggression. *Psychology of Men & Masculinity, 16*(2), 160–169. https://doi.org/10.1037/a0035956

Sobočan, A. M. (2011). Female same-sex families in the dialectics of marginality and conformity. *Journal of Lesbian Studies, 15*(3), 384–405. https://doi.org/10.1080/10894160.2011.530157

Specia, M. (2019, November 1). Threats and abuse prompt female lawmakers to leave U.K. Parliament. *The New York Times.* www.nytimes.com/2019/11/01/world/europe/women-parliament-abuse.html?auth=login-email&login=email

Stöckl, H., Devries, K., Rotstein, A., Abrahams, N., Campbell, J., Watts, C., & Moreno, C. G. (2013). The global prevalence of intimate partner homicide: A systematic review. *The Lancet, 382*(9895), 859–865. https://doi.org/10.1016/S0140-6736(13)61030-2

Sudarkasa, N. (2004). Conceptions of motherhood in nuclear and extended families, with special reference to comparative studies involving African societies. *JENdA: A Journal of Culture and African Women Studies, 5.* Retrieved January 19, 2009, from coNquiS92 http://www.jendajournal.com/issue5/sudarkasa.htm

Swami, V. (2015). Cultural influences on body size ideals: Unpacking the impact of westernization and modernization. *European Psychologist, 20*, 44–51. http://doi.org/10.1027/1016-9040/a000150.

Swami, V., Frederick, D. A., Aavik, T., Alcalay, L., Allik, J., Anderson, D., et al. (2010). The attractive female body weight and female body dissatisfaction in 26 countries across 10 world regions: Results of the International Body Project I. *Personality and Social Psychology Bulletin, 36*, 309–325. http://doi.org/10.1177/0146167209359702

Swami, V., Miah, J., Noorani, N., & Taylor, D. (2014). Is the hijab protective? An investigation of body image and related constructs among British Muslim women. *British Journal of Psychology, 105*, 352–363. http://doi.org/10.1111/bjop.12045

Tanaka, C. T., Berger, W., Valença, A. M., Coutinho, E. S. F., Jean-Louis, G., Fontenelle, L. F., & Mendlowicz, M. V.. (2017). The worldwide incidence of neonaticide: A systematic review. *Archives of Women's Mental Health, 20*(2), 249–256. https://doi.org/10.1007/s00737-016-0703-8

Taub, A. (2020, April 6). A new COVID-19 crisis: Domestic abuse rises worldwide. *The New York Times*. www.nytimes.com/2020/04/06/world/coronavirus-domestic-violence.html

Thomas-Hunt, M. C., & Phillips, K. W. (2004). When what you know is not enough: Expertise and gender dynamics in task groups. *Personality and Social Psychology Bulletin, 30*(12), 1585–1598. https://doi.org/10.1177/0146167204271186

Tiggemann, M. (2004). Body image across the life span: Stability and change. *Body Image, 1*, 29–41.

Tiggemann, M. (2015). Considerations of positive body image across various social identities and special populations. *Body Image, 14*, 168–176. https://doi.org/10.1016/j.bodyim.2015.03.002

Ting, J.Y., & Hwang, W. C. (2007). Eating disorders in Asian American women: Integrating multiculturalism and feminism. *Women & Therapy, 30*, 145–160.

Tolman, D. L., & Chmielewski, J. F. (2019). From tightrope to minefield: How the sexual double standard "lives" in adolescent girls' and young women's lives. In S. Lamb & J. Gilbert (Eds.), *Cambridge handbooks in psychology. The Cambridge handbook of sexual development: Childhood and adolescence* (p. 198–220). Cambridge University Press.

Turton, S. (2017, July 21). Bosnian war rape survivors speak of their suffering 25 years on. *Independent*. www.independent.co.uk/news/long_reads/bosnia-war-rape-survivors-speak-serbian-soldiers-balkans-women-justice-suffering-a7846546.html

Uecker, J. E., & Martinez, B. C. (2017). When and why women regret sex in hookups more than men do: An analysis of the online college social life survey. *The Sociological Quarterly, 58*, 470–494. http://dx.doi.org/10.1080/00380253.2017.1331716

UN Women (2019, December 11). International Women's Day 2020 theme – "I am Generation Equality: Realizing Women's Rights." www.unwomen .org/en/news/stories/2019/12/announcer-international-womens-day-2020-theme

UNICEF (2013, July). *Female genital mutilation/cutting: A statistical overview and exploration of the dynamics of change.* New York: Author. file:///C:/ Users/hlips/AppData/Local/Temp/FGMC_Lo_res_Final_26.pdf

United Nations. (1997, May 23). *Fourth World Conference on Women (1995).* www.un.org/geninfo/bp/women.html

United Nations Development Programme (2019). *Gender Inequality Index (GII).* http://hdr.undp.org/en/indicators/68606

United Nations Office on Drugs and Crime (2018). *Global report on trafficking in persons 2018.* Vienna: Author. www.unodc.org/documents/data-and-ana lysis/glotip/2018/GLOTiP_2018_BOOK_web_small.pdf

US Bureau of Labor Statistics (2018b). News release. American Time Use Survey – 2017 results. www.bls.gov/news.release/pdf/atus.pdf

US Census Bureau, Historical Income Tables (2019). Table P-36: Full-time, year-round all workers by median income and sex: 1955 to 2016. www.census.gov/data/tables/time-series/demo/income-poverty/historical-income-people.html

US Department of Labor (n.d.). Title IX, education amendments of 1972. www .dol.gov/oasam/regs/statutes/titleIX.htm

VanderEnde, K. E., Yount, K. M., Dynes, M. M., & Sibley, L. M. (2012). Community-level correlates of intimate partner violence against women globally: A systematic review. *Social Science & Medicine, 75* (7), 1143–1155. https://doi.org/10.1016/j.socscimed.2012.05.027

Van Osch, Y. M. J., Breugelmans, S. M., Zeelenberg, M., & Bölük, P. (2013). A different kind of honor culture: Family honor and aggression in Turks. *Group Processes & Intergroup Relations, 16,* 334–344. http://doi.org/ 10.1177/1368430212467475.

van Veelen, R., Derks, B., & Endedijk, M. D. (2019). Double trouble: How being outnumbered and negatively stereotyped threatens career outcomes of women in stem. *Frontiers in Psychology, 10,* Article 150. https://doi.org/ 10.3389/fpsyg.2019.00150

Verniers, C., & Vala, J. (2018). Justifying gender discrimination in the work-place: The mediating role of motherhood myths. *PLoS ONE, 13*(1): e0190657. https://doi.org/10.1371/journal.pone.0190657

Vial, A. C., Napier, J. L., & Brescoll, V. L. (2016). A bed of thorns: Female leaders and the self-reinforcing cycle of illegitimacy. *The Leadership Quarterly, 27*(3), 400–414. https://doi.org/10.1016/j.leaqua.2015.12.004

Vives-Cases, C., La Parra, D., Goicolea, I., Felt, E., Briones-Vozmediano, E., Ortiz-Barreda, G., & Gil-González, G. (2014). *Preventing and addressing intimate partner violence against migrant and ethnic minority women:Tthe role of the health sector.* Copenhagen: World Health Organization. www.euro.who.int/__data/assets/pdf_file/0018/270180/21256-WHO-Intimate-Partner-Violence_low_V7.pdf?ua=1

Voolma, H. (2018). "I must be silent because of residency": Barriers to escaping domestic violence in the context of insecure immigration status in England and Sweden. *Violence against Women, 24*(15), 1830–1850. https://doi.org/10.1177/1077801218755974

Wang, M., Yogeeswaran, K., Andrews, N. P., Hawi, D. R., & Sibley, C. G. (2019). How common is cyberbullying among adults? Exploring gender, ethnic, and age differences in the prevalence of cyberbullying. *Cyberpsychology, Behavior, and Social Networking, 22*(11). Published online. https://doi.org/10.1089/cyber.2019.0146

Watts, C., & Zimmerman, C. (2002). Violence against women: Global scope and magnitude. *The Lancet, 359*(9313), 1232–1237. https://doi.org/10.1016/S0140-6736(02)08221-1

Weller, C. (2014, August 24). These 10 countries have the best parental leave policies in the world. *World Economic Forum.* www.weforum.org/agenda/2016/08/these-10-countries-have-the-best-parental-leave-policies-in-the-world

Westminster Foundation for Democracy (2018, March). *Violence against women in politics: Global perspectives on a global issue.* www.wfd.org/wp-content/uploads/2018/04/Violence-Against-Women-in-Politics-Global-Perspectives-of-a-Global-Issue.pdf

Whyte, S., Brooks, R. C., & Torgler, B. (2018). Man, woman, "other": Factors associated with nonbinary gender identification. *Archives of Sexual Behavior, 47*(8), 2397–2406. https://doi.org/10.1007/s10508-018-1307-3

Willer, R., Rogalin, C. L., Conlon, B., & Wojnowicz, M. T. (2013). Overdoing gender: A test of the masculine overcompensation thesis. *American Journal of Sociology, 118*(4), 980–1022. https://doi.org/10.1086/668417

Willemsen, T. M. (2002). Gender typing of the successful manager-A stereotype reconsidered. *Sex Roles: A Journal of Research, 46*(11–12), 385–391. https://doi.org/10.1023/A:1020409429645

Williams, M. J., & Tiedens, L. Z. (2016). The subtle suspension of backlash: A meta-analysis of penalties for women's implicit and explicit dominance behavior. *Psychological Bulletin, 142*(2), 165–197. https://doi.org/10.1037/bul0000039

Williams, S. L., McKelvey, D. K., & Frieze, I. H. (2014). *Intimate-partner violence.* In R. Gartner & B. McCarthy (Eds.), *The Oxford handbooks in criminology and criminal justice. The Oxford handbook of gender, sex, and crime* (p. 362–378). Oxford University Press.

Wilson, S. (2007). "When you have children, you're obliged to live": motherhood, chronic illness and biographical disruption. *Sociology of Health & Illness, 29*, 610–625.

World Bank (2020). Labor force participation rate, female. https://data.world bank.org/indicator/SL.TLF.CACT.FE.ZS

World Economic Forum (2019). *Global Gender Gap Report 2020*. Geneva, Switzerland. www3.weforum.org/docs/WEF_GGGR_2020.pdf

Yardley, J. & Bagri, N. T. (2013). Notorious attack spurs India to approve new rape laws. *New York Times*. www.nytimes.com/2013/02/04/world/asia/india-approves-tougher-rape-laws.html

Yim, I. S., & Kofman, Y. B. (2019). The psychobiology of stress and intimate partner violence. *Psychoneuroendocrinology, 105*, 9–24. https://doi.org/10.1016/j.psyneuen.2018.08.017

Yoder, J. D., Schleicher, T. L., & McDonald, T. W. (1998). Empowering token women leaders: The importance of organizationally legitimated credibility. *Psychology of Women Quarterly, 22*(2), 209–222. https://doi.org/10.1111/J.1471-6402.1998.tb00151.x

Yoon, E., Adams, K., Hogge, I., Bruner, J. P., Surya, S., & Bryant, F. B. (2015). Development and validation of the Patriarchal Beliefs Scale. *Journal of Counseling Psychology, 62*, 264–279. https://doi.org/10.1037/cou0000056

Yoon, E., Cabirou, L., Bhang, C., & Galvin, S. (2019). Acculturation and patriarchal beliefs among Asian American young adults: A preliminary investigation. *Asian American Journal of Psychology, 10*(2), 122–130. https://doi.org/10.1037/aap0000130

You, S., & Shin, K. (2020). Influence of patriarchal sex-role attitudes on perpetration of dating violence. *Current Psychology: A Journal for Diverse Perspectives on Diverse Psychological Issues*. Advance online publication. https://doi.org/10.1007/s12144-020-00632-4

Yu, J., & Xie, Y. (2018). Motherhood penalties and living arrangements in China. *Journal of Marriage and Family, 80*(5), 1067–1086. https://doi.org/10.1111/jomf.12496

Yun, R. J., & Lachman, M. E. (2006). Perceptions of aging in two cultures: Korean and American views on old age. *Journal of Cross-Cultural Gerontology, 21*, 55–70. http://doi.org/10.1007/s10823-006-9018-y.

Zhabenko, A. (2019). Russian lesbian mothers: Between "traditional values" and human rights. *Journal of Lesbian Studies, 23*(3), 321–335. https://doi.org/10.1080/10894160.2019.1598207

# Cambridge Elements ≡

# Psychology and Culture

## Kenneth D. Keith

*University of San Diego*

Kenneth D. Keith is author or editor of more than 160 publications on cross-cultural psychology, quality of life, intellectual disability, and the teaching of psychology. He was the 2017 president of the Society for the Teaching of Psychology.

## About the Series

*Elements in Psychology and Culture* features authoritative surveys and updates on key topics in cultural, cross-cultural, and indigenous psychology. Authors are internationally recognized scholars whose work is at the forefront of their subdisciplines within the realm of psychology and culture.

Cambridge Elements ≡

# Psychology and Culture

## Elements in the Series

Printed in the United States
By Bookmasters